World Famous Landmarks

By
Cynthia Adams

Cover Design by
Annette Hollister-Papp

Cover Illustrations by
Jane Burns

Inside Illustrations by
Marc F. Johnson

Publishers
Instructional Fair • TS Denison
Grand Rapids, Michigan 49544

Dedication
To Paul who means the world to me

Credits
Author: Cynthia G. Adams
Cover Illustrations: Jane Burns
Cover Art Direction: Annette Hollister-Papp
Poster Art Direction: Annette Hollister-Papp,
     Matthew Van Zomeren
Inside Illustrations: Marc F. Johnson
Project Director: Danielle de Gregory
Editors: Danielle de Gregory, Debra Olson Pressnall
Graphic Design/Layout: Deborah Hanson McNiff

About the Author
Cynthia G. Adams, M.Ed., is a graduate of the University of Cincinnati and Xavier University in Cincinnati, Ohio. She has taught elementary music and special education in Cincinnati public schools for 24 years. In addition, Cynthia G. Adams has been a presenter at local thematic teaching seminars.

Standard Book Number: 1-56822-674-8
World Famous Landmarks
Cover and Poster Photographs © Corel Corporation
Copyright © 1998 by Instructional Fair • TS Denison
2400 Turner Avenue NW
Grand Rapids, Michigan 49544

All Rights Reserved • Printed in the USA

Introduction

World Famous Landmarks is a perfect compliment for your units of study on the continents! *World Famous Landmarks* provides enough information and activity suggestions for students to learn how to make connections to the real world, past and present, as well as encouraging them to delve into independent research. You can use the materials in *World Famous Landmarks* to visit these fascinating landmarks and discover history, art, architecture, math, science, and social studies. Set up your social studies learning center by displaying the four colorful posters that feature beautiful photographs. The reproducible information sheets, web site addresses, and activities pages in *World Famous Landmarks* make the creation of your social studies learning center a quick, no-fuss task.

Divided into four continental regions, *World Famous Landmarks* includes a description of each continental area before launching the student into an exploration of a landmark and local points of interest. In the back of the book you will find a beautiful poster for each continental region. These one-sided color posters can easily be pulled out and displayed to show your students images of some of the landmarks, as well as a map with landmark locations to enable students to comprehend geographic relationships.

This resource is intended to help you give your students an understanding of the amazing variety of both natural and constructed landmarks throughout our world. Fifty-five specific landmarks are described and explored. You can introduce your students to a particular structure with the reproducible information page. Not only do these information pages give interesting and important information about landmarks, they also treat each landmark as a starting point to learn about cultures, geography, science, art, architecture, and a wealth of other subjects. Each of the information pages contains a few questions, some of which may be answered by carefully reading the page, others require further research in order to challenge your students. Vocabulary words are printed in boldface type to alert you and your students to an avenue of language arts that might need to be researched.

In addition, for each landmark, the author of *World Famous Landmarks* has provided a web site address to further explore and to encourage computer and "web surfing" skills. *Note:* Because of the mutable nature of the Internet, web sites do change. The sites listed in this resource were current at the time of publication.

Following the information page for each landmark is a reproducible page with four activities, ready to be cut out and attached to index cards for easy filing in a learning center. These projects can be approached individually or as a team effort. Each of the four activities indicates for which curriculum area it is most appropriate.

To complete your social studies learning center on a particular landmark, a third reproducible activity page offers a variety of activities—research projects, mazes, crossword puzzles, word searches, or creative writing and drawing exercises.

At the end of *World Famous Landmarks*, a quick reference list of *National Geographic* resources with photographic examples of some of the landmarks is provided. If the reference includes any photographs that might cause "undue attention" from students, a note regarding the content of the pictures is included next to the reference.

The *Circling the World* series was developed to encourage students to approach learning using their natural curiosity. An interesting subject naturally invites questions that explore links to other areas and subjects. Discussions about people and places, experiments that spring from a fascinating building material or era, and visual images—all ensure that students remain fascinated by the world and excited to explore a myriad of learning possibilities.

Table of Contents

Africa

Africa 6
The Great Pyramid 7
   Center Projects 8
   Mummification 9
The Great Rift Valley 10
   Center Projects 11
   Plate Tectonics 12
The Great Zimbabwe 13
   Center Projects 14
   The Great Zimbabwe 15
The Mosque at Djenne 16
   Center Projects 17
   Mud Construction 18
Mount Kilimanjaro 19
   Center Projects 20
   Mountains of the World 21
The Aswan High Dam and the Nile River 22
   Center Projects 23
   The Aswan High Dam and the Nile River ...24
The Sahara Desert 25
   Center Projects 26
   The Sahara Desert 27
Serengeti National Park 28
   Center Projects 29
   Serengeti National Park 30
The Suez Canal 31
   Center Projects 32
   International Trade 33

Asia, Australia, New Zealand

Asia, Australia, New Zealand 34
Al-Haram and Mecca 35
   Center Projects 36
   Al-Haram and Mecca 37
Angkor Wat 38
   Center Projects 39
   A Do-It-Yourself Jungle Expedition 40
Uluru (Ayers Rock) 41
   Center Projects 42
   Word Search Puzzle 43
The Dead Sea 44
   Center Projects 45
   Current Events Summary Form 46

The Forbidden City 47
   Center Projects 48
   The Forbidden City 49
The Grand Palace 50
   Center Projects 51
   The Grand Palace 52
The Great Barrier Reef 53
   Center Projects 54
   The Great Barrier Reef 55
The Great Wall of China 56
   Center Projects 57
   The Great Wall of China 58
Healesville Wildlife Sanctuary 59
   Center Projects 60
   Australia's Animals 61
The Imperial Palace 62
   Center Projects 63
   The Imperial Palace 64
Kansai Airport 65
   Center Projects 66
   Kansai Airport 67
Lake Baikal 68
   Center Projects 69
   Lake Baikal 70
Mount Everest 71
   Center Projects 72
   Mount Everest 73
Shwe Dagon Pagoda 74
   Center Projects 75
   Shwe Dagon Pagoda 76
Sydney Opera House 77
   Center Projects 78
   Sydney Opera House 79
The Taj Mahal 80
   Center Projects 81
   The Taj Mahal 82
The Waiotapu Thermal Wonderland 83
   Center Projects 84
   Word Search Puzzle 85

Europe

Europe 86
The Alhambra 87
   Center Projects 88
   The Alhambra 89

Table of Contents

The Channel Tunnel 90
   Center Projects 91
   Word Search Puzzle 92
The Colosseum 93
   Center Projects 94
   The Colosseum 95
The Eiffel Tower 96
   Center Projects 97
   Crossword Puzzle 98
Hagia Sophia 99
   Center Projects 100
   Hagia Sophia 101
The Kremlin 102
   Center Projects 103
   Crossword Puzzle 104
Neuschwanstein Castle 105
   Center Projects 106
   Neuschwanstein Castle 107
The Parthenon 108
   Center Projects 109
   The Parthenon 110
The Sognefjorden 111
   Center Projects 112
   The Sognefjorden 113
Stonehenge 114
   Center Projects 115
   Crossword Puzzle 116
The Tower of London and Tower Bridge 117
   Center Projects 118
   The Ravens 119
Vatican City 120
   Center Projects 121
   Vatican City 122
Venice 123
   Center Projects 124
   Venice 125
The Vienna State Opera House 126
   Center Projects 127
   The Vienna State Opera House 128

North and South America

North and South America 129
The Amazon Rain Forest 130
   Center Projects 131
   Addressing the Issue 132

Brasília 133
   Center Projects 134
   Brasília 135
Chichén Itzá 136
   Center Projects 137
   Chichén Itzá 138
The CN Tower 139
   Center Projects 140
   The CN Tower 141
Easter Island 142
   Center Projects 143
   Can You Solve the Mystery? 144
The Galapagos Islands 145
   Center Projects 146
   The Galapagos Islands 147
The Golden Gate Bridge 148
   Center Projects 149
   The Golden Gate Bridge 150
The Grand Canyon National Park 151
   Center Projects 152
   The Grand Canyon National Park 153
Hoover Dam 154
   Center Projects 155
   Hoover Dam 156
Machu Picchu 157
   Center Projects 158
   Machu Picchu 159
Mauna Loa 160
   Center Projects 161
   Mauna Loa 162
Mesa Verde 163
   Center Projects 164
   Mesa Verde 165
The Panama Canal 166
   Center Projects 167
   Tracing the Journey 168
The Statue of Liberty 169
   Center Projects 170
   Crayon Resist Picture 171
Tenochtitlán 172
   Center Projects 173
   Tenochtitlán 174
Reference List 175
Answer Key 176

Africa

Africa is the second largest continent. It has 53 independent countries and several political units. It is a continent of contrast, with untouched natural beauty and modern cities, rain forests and deserts.

In the early 1900s, Europeans colonized Africa in order to control its valuable resources. Africans fought the European takeover and by the middle of the century many of the colonies were independent. Unfortunately, many leaders of the new nations were not prepared for the economic and social problems that followed. In some cases, military officers overthrew the new governments and created dictatorships. Wars among culture groups still threaten the continent.

The six countries of northern Africa have close ties to Europe and the Middle East. They form a region apart from the African countries south of the Sahara. Most of the people living in Mauritania, Morocco, Algeria, Tunisia, Libya, and Egypt speak Arabic and practice the Islamic religion.

There are about 731 million people in Africa today. Three-fourths of them are members of culture groups with the same religion, language, and traditions. Most of the people live in rural areas, earning money by growing crops or raising livestock. Others have moved to the cities for better jobs and a modern way of life. Many African countries need foreign aid to support their people.

Africa produces most of the world's supply of cassava, cocoa beans, and yams. There are also large deposits of copper, diamonds, gold, and petroleum. Tourists, drawn to the continent because of its wildlife, are important to the economy of Africa. Wildlife, including giraffes, elephants, lions, and zebras, live on the grasslands of eastern and southern Africa.

The continent has the world's longest river, the Nile, the largest desert, the Sahara, and the highest single mountain, Mount Kilimanjaro.

The Great Pyramid

When it was built, the Great **Pyramid**, a tomb for the **Pharaoh** Cheops, was the tallest structure in the world. It is 480 feet high (146 m) and took more than 20 years to complete. There are several smaller pyramids and two temples still standing with the Great Pyramid at Giza, Egypt.

The Great Pyramid contains two and a half million blocks of **limestone** and **granite**. Each block weighs more than two tons. The base of the pyramid covers 13 acres (755 feet or 230 meters) on each side. It is as high as a 40-story building. **Archaeologists** have learned a great deal about ancient Egyptians by studying the pyramids.

It is believed that building the structure required the labor of thousands of people and took 20 to 30 years to complete. After a priest determined true north to position the pyramid, workers prepared the ground to make a level base. Before any construction began, **masons** dug underground chambers, one of which would hold the pharaoh's **sarcophagus**. A strong roof was built over the **burial chamber**, then the **cornerstones** were put in place and the main blocks were laid on the base. A network of passages was built into the many layers of stone block which were moved into place with a system of levers, rollers, and planks. Finally, the granite **capstone** was added to the top.

Ancient Egyptians believed that people who died lived in an **afterlife**. They removed the organs from the bodies and wrapped them in linen cloth. Food, clothing, furniture, and jewelry were buried with the body.

Answer in complete sentences:

1. What structures are standing in the cemetery at Giza, Egypt?

2. What were the steps to building the Great Pyramid?

3. How was it possible for the Egyptians to move the heavy stones without wheels?

4. What were some ancient Egyptian beliefs about an afterlife?

5. What famous part-human and part-animal statue is located at Giza?

Web Site:
www.citi.net/home/egypt/links/pyramid.html

Creative Writing

You will need:
- ✔ nonfiction books about pyramids around the world
- ✔ paper
- ✔ pencil

The ancient cultures of South and Central America also built pyramids. Do you think they could have known about the Egyptian pyramids? Give reasons to support your answer.

Art

You will need:
- ✔ paper
- ✔ pencil
- ✔ markers

Heiroglyphics were carved into stone or painted on the walls of tombs. Work with a partner to create a system of picture writing like the Egyptians used. Create a different symbol for each letter of the alphabet. Using these symbols, print your name and the names of your family members.

Science

You will need:
- ✔ 12 unsharpened pencils
- ✔ string
- ✔ two rulers
- ✔ several differently-sized wooden blocks

Demonstrate the Egyptian method for moving heavy stone blocks by using the pencils as rollers, the string for rope, and the rulers as levers. What simple machines were the Egyptians using?

Research

You will need:
- ✔ encyclopedia (volume T)
- ✔ paper
- ✔ pencil

Read about another Egyptian king named Tutankhamen. He became king at age nine and died at eighteen. Make a list of the contents of his four-room tomb.

The Great Pyramid
Mummification

Ancient Egyptians were mummified after death. The process, which took about 70 days, was done by special priests. The body was laid under a canopy and taken to the burial site. Priests washed the corpse and rubbed the body with *natron* (a kind of salt) to dry and preserve the skin. They coated the face with resin to protect it. A priest removed the lungs, liver, stomach, and intestines and stored them in separate jars. The body was then stuffed full of bandages, resin, sawdust, and natron. After this, each part of the body was bandaged separately. Finally, the head was painted green and a lifelike face was added.

Choose one:

▲ If you could omit one step in the mummification process, which would it be? Explain your choice.

▲ Invent a new, simpler procedure that would effectively preserve bodies. Write at least five steps.

▲ Select one step of the mummification process and write about your impressions as if you were there. Make an illustration.

▲ Read and summarize the myth of Osiris, believed to be the basis for the mummification ceremony. You can find information in *The Facts on File Encyclopedia of World Mythology and Legends* by Anthony S. Mercatante, 1988, or *MUMMIES: A Very Peculiar History* by Nathaniel Harris, Watts, 1995.

The Great Rift Valley

The Great Rift Valley was carved from the land millions of years ago. The Rift runs down the entire African continent. It is 4,000 miles (6,437 km) long. The area includes **vertical canyon** walls as high as 6,600 feet (2,011 m) and broad valleys as much as 60 miles (97 km) wide. On a clear day, the **rift** can be seen from the moon.

Scientists believe that the valley was formed when the earth's outer shell moved. The rock layers of earth moved and spread apart. Over time they crashed into each other. These movements created the Great Rift Valley. **Erosion** and volcanoes also helped shape the land.

There is much life, both **primitive** and modern, in the Great Rift Valley. Lake Naivasha is home to 400 species of birds. Flowers and vegetables grow well in the **fertile** volcanic soil. The Masai Mara National Park is a wildlife preserve in Kenya. Many tourists go there on **safari.**

Some of the earliest known human remains have been found in the Great Rift Valley. Anthropologists Louis and Mary Leakey found fragments of bones, teeth, and tools about two million years old. The Leakeys guessed that humankind probably had its start in East Africa.

Answer in complete sentences:

1. Who were Louis and Mary Leakey?

2. What is the job of an anthropologist? an archaeologist?

3. What are the landforms of the Great Rift Valley?

4. How do scientists believe the valley was formed?

5. What is special about Lake Naivasha?

Web site:
www.kenyaweb.com/

Creative Writing

You will need:
- ✔ research information about Tanzania's Olduvai Gorge, Louis and Mary Leakey
- ✔ pencil
- ✔ paper

Write a one-week diary explaining discoveries made by the Leakeys at the Gorge.

Geography

You will need:
- ✔ map of Africa
- ✔ pencil
- ✔ atlas
- ✔ almanac

Trace the Great Rift Valley through eastern Africa from Ethiopia to Mozambique.

What modern cities lie within the Great Rift Valley? Rank the cities from largest to smallest.

Social Studies

You will need:
- ✔ art supplies
- ✔ reference materials

Draw a large map of Africa and design a game path along the line of the Great Rift Valley. Write questions about the continent that must be answered to move along the path and win the game.

Science

You will need:
- ✔ encyclopedia (volume P)
- ✔ paper
- ✔ pencil
- ✔ art supplies
- ✔ towels

How does the Plate Tectonics Theory explain the formation of the Great Rift Valley? Using towels, create a model to demonstrate how the Great Rift Valley was formed.

The Great Rift Valley

Plate Tectonics

The Great Rift Valley was formed when the earth's outer shell moved. The rate of movement was very slow [about 4 inches (10 cm) a year] but it has been going on for millions of years. Scientists believe that in time a sea will form as the gaps in the earth fill with water.

Define:

tectonic plates _____

_____

crust_____

_____

mantle _____

_____

lithosphere _____

_____

asthenosphere _____

_____

Label the terms on this diagram.

The Great Zimbabwe

Archaeologists believe that the stone ruins known as the Great Zimbabwe were once the center of a great African **empire**. Remains of houses and stone **enclosures** from the eighth century have been found. The empire was at its height from the 12th to the 15th centuries. It is known that the Shona tribe of Mozambique and Zimbabwe ruled the area from about 1100. The name Zimbabwe means "stone houses" in the Bantu language.

A large circular stone wall is still standing at the **site** and the **foundations** of mud buildings and a round stone tower 30 feet (9 m) tall are still inside the main wall. Nearby is a hill that was probably used as a **fortress** and the **remnants** of several smaller enclosures.

It is known that the first people to live at the Great Zimbabwe were cattle breeders and farmers. They mined and traded gold with the Arabs and Chinese. Their **port** on the Indian Ocean was used for trade with Europe. Written **evidence** from European traders in the 16th century shows a highly developed society. Great Zimbabwe was discovered by Europeans in 1867. It is thought that the city failed because of **drought** and **famine**.

Answer in complete sentences:

1. What remains of Great Zimbabwe?

2. What were the occupations of the original settlers?

3. What physical evidence might have led archaeologists to draw their conclusions about the civilization at Great Zimbabwe?

4. Why would a city suffering a drought also experience famine?

Web site:
www.africaonline.com/AfricaOnline/travel/zimbabwe/attractions.html

Creative Writing

You will need:
- ✔ writing paper
- ✔ drawing paper
- ✔ pencil
- ✔ markers

Write a story and make a drawing showing what life might have been like for a family living inside the walls of Great Zimbabwe.

Creative Writing

You will need:
- ✔ paper
- ✔ pencil

Who would have been more important to the community at Great Zimbabwe, the farmers and cattle breeders or the people who traded with the Arabs and Chinese? Explain.

Science

You will need:
- ✔ nonfiction information about weather conditions and agriculture in Africa
- ✔ paper
- ✔ pencil

What modern technology might have saved the people of Great Zimbabwe from famine? What crops can be grown in drought conditions?

How do weather conditions affect the stone ruins of the Great Zimbabwe?

Art

You will need:
- ✔ nonfiction books about Zimbabwe and Mozambique
- ✔ paper
- ✔ drawing pencils

Make drawings of homes in Zimbabwe and Mozambique. How are they like or unlike the huts in Great Zimbabwe?

The Great Zimbabwe

A round stone tower 30 feet high (9 m) still stands inside the Great Enclosure. It is made without mortar to hold it in place. Think of what you have learned about the Zimbabwe civilization. For what might the tower have been used?

Write your ideas and complete the cutaway drawing.

Bonus Persuade a friend that your ideas are true.

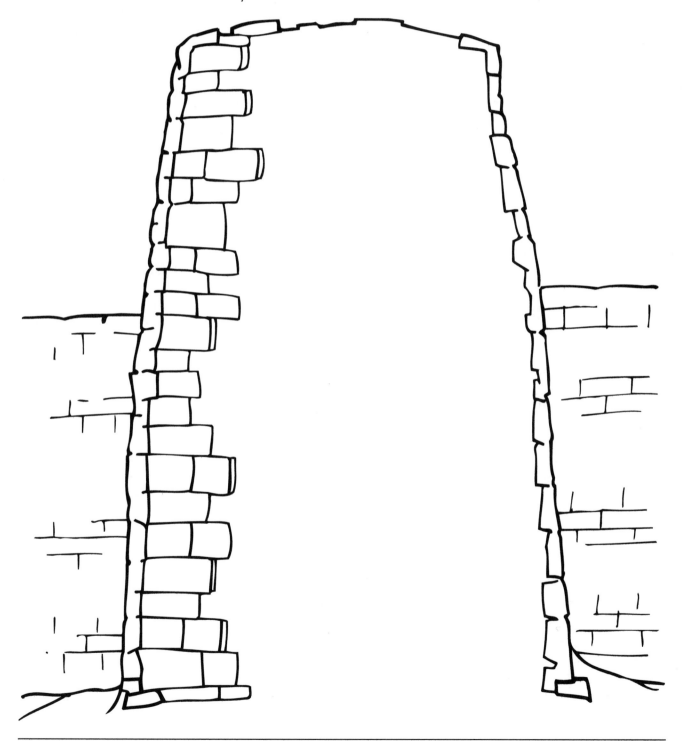

The Mosque at Djenne

The Grand Mosque, located in Djenne, Mali, in West Africa, was completed in 1907. It is the largest example of mud construction in the world. Located in south central Mali, Djenne has about 8,000 **residents**. The city was once a busy marketplace and a center for the Islamic religion.

The mosque was built in the Sudan style with small windows and heavy walls to **insulate** against the hot days and cold nights. **Rice** or **millet hulls** were mixed with the mud to make it rain **resistant**. The thick walls are made of **adobe** bricks. A layer of mud on the bricks gives the mosque a molded look.

Gutters made of fired clay pipes move water off the roofs without damaging the sides of the building. The mosque still must be repaired each year when the outside becomes softened by rain. Local people sell crafts and food to visitors on a **plaza** outside the Grand Mosque.

Answer in complete sentences:

1. How was the mosque built to protect against weather?

2. Where is Djenne located?

3. Why do you think this mosque is built of mud?

4. How do local people earn money near the Grand Mosque?

Web site:
cc.emory.edu/HART/HART101/African/Review.html

Creative Writing

You will need:
- paper
- pencil

Write a letter to a friend that would convince him or her to visit the Grand Mosque while touring West Africa.

Social Studies

You will need:
- Mali coat of arms
- nonfiction information about Mali
- paper
- red, yellow, black, and green markers
- pencil

Copy the coat of arms for the Republic of Mali. Why is the mosque pictured on the coat of arms? Explain the meaning of each symbol. Why do Malians speak French?

Social Studies

You will need:
- nonfiction information about Africa and Islam
- paper
- pencil

Name the six countries of Northern Africa where Islam is the main religion. What are some other religions that are practiced in those countries?

Science

You will need:
- nonfiction information about Mali, West Africa
- paper
- pencil

Describe how seasonal weather changes would affect the Grand Mosque. What challenges must the people of Mali endure because of unpredictable amounts of rainfall? How does the mosque at Djenne differ from two other mosques around the world?

The Mosque at Djenne

Mud Construction

Nearly half of the world's population live in mud structures. This method of building is most appropriate in areas with little rainfall and warm temperatures. Mud construction requires many workers for regular repairs and is most common in countries with an agricultural economy.

Answer these questions:

1. Why is mud construction well-suited to Africa? _____

   _____

   _____

2. What maintenance is necessary on mud structures? How do the people deal with these problems? _____

   _____

   _____

3. Why is wood and brick construction not as common? _____

   _____

   _____

4. How would you be protected from the heat and rainfall in a mud house? _____

   _____

   _____

5. Draw your idea for a house made from mud. Describe your home.

   - How would you gather the materials?
   - How would you form the bricks?
   - How would you create windows and doors?

   _____

   _____

   _____

   _____

   _____

   _____

Mount Kilimanjaro

Mount Kilimanjaro is the highest mountain in Africa. It is on the border between Tanzania and Kenya. There are two **peaks**. Kibo, the higher peak, is always covered with snow. It is shaped like a volcano with a deep **crater**. There are **glaciers** around the rim of the volcano. Mawensi, the other peak, has no snow. The highest point is Uhuru Peak. Kilimanjaro is one of a group of **dormant** volcanoes formed about the same time as the Great Rift Valley.

Farmers use the rich soil and heavy **rainfall** of Mount Kilimanjaro to grow bananas, coffee, and vegetables. The area is also a popular spot for tourists. Kilimanjaro National Park is at the bottom of the mountain and contains **scenic** forests that are home to several species of **endangered** animals.

Kilimanjaro was "discovered" by German missionaries in 1848. Hans Meyer was the first European to climb Kibo in 1889 and Mawensi was climbed by Fritz Klut in 1912.

Answer in complete sentences:

1. Name the two peaks of Mount Kilimanjaro. What is the highest point called?
2. What crops are grown near Mount Kilimanjaro?
3. Who were the first Europeans to climb Kibo and Mawensi?
4. Why is the area around Mount Kilimanjaro popular with tourists?

Web site:
www-genome.wi.mit.edu/~carl/kilisaver/slide8medium20.html

Science

You will need:
- ✔ paper
- ✔ pencil
- ✔ nonfiction materials about mountain climbers

Read about mountain climbers. Suppose you were going to climb Mount Kilimanjaro. How would you get in shape before attempting such a climb? What supplies would you need? How would you dress? What safety precautions would be necessary?

Research

You will need:
- ✔ encyclopedia (volume G)
- ✔ paper
- ✔ pencil

What is the job of a geologist? What do we learn from a geologist's study of mountains?

Math

You will need:
- ✔ encyclopedia (volume K)
- ✔ paper
- ✔ pencil

How tall is each peak (Kibo and Mawensi) in feet and meters? What is the average of the two?

Science

You will need:
- ✔ nonfiction books about Tanzania and Kenya
- ✔ paper
- ✔ pencil

Read about one of the endangered animals that live in Kilimanjaro National Park. Write a paragraph and make a drawing. Explain how the animal is able to live in the mountains and why it is endangered.

Mount Kilimanjaro

Mountains of the World

Use an encyclopedia or reference book to complete this chart.

	Location country—hemisphere	Height feet—meters
Mount Kilimanjaro		
Mauna Loa		
Mount Fuji		
Mount Everest		
Mount Olympus		
Matterhorn		

The Aswan High Dam and the Nile River

The Nile is the longest river in the world. It flows through northeast Africa into the Mediterranean Sea for a distance of 4,145 miles (6,669 km). Water from the Nile **irrigates** farmland in Egypt and Sudan. People swim, bathe, and wash their clothes in the waters of the Nile. North of Cairo, Egypt, the river divides into separate **channels**, creating areas of **swamp**, salt lakes, and fertile soil in the Nile **Delta**. The river floods areas of the delta every summer.

The Aswan High Dam was completed in 1970. It was necessary to control the Nile River in order to stop the flooding. The dam is 2.3 miles (3.26 km) long and 364 feet (111 m) high. The **reservoir** (Lake Nassar) formed above the dam provides water for irrigation and power for electricity. The cost of building the dam made of **granite** rock-fill, clay, earth, and cement was more than one billion dollars. Some of the money came from the Soviet Union.

Fifty thousand people had to be moved because of the dam. Two ancient Egyptian temples were taken apart, moved, and rebuilt.

Unfortunately, the dam has caused several environmental problems. When the flood waters were stopped, fertile **silt** was no longer **deposited** on the farmland. Farmers now use chemical **fertilizers**. Without the silt, **erosion** is occurring on the land near the Mediterranean coast.

There has also been an increase in a disease called schistosomiasis. It is caused by tiny worms that live in snails that breed in the waters of the Nile. Before the dam, the river bed dried up every year and the snails died. Finally, the rise in the water table has brought salts to the surface, making some of the surrounding soil **infertile**.

Answer in complete sentences:

1. What is the name of the reservoir created by the Aswan High Dam?

2. How long is the Nile River and where is it located?

3. How does a dam benefit an area?

4. What materials were used to make the Aswan High Dam?

5. How does silt benefit farmers?

Web site:
163.121.10.41/tourism/docs/aswam/hidam.htm

Social Studies

You will need:
- chart paper
- marker

Divide the paper in half. Make a list of ways the dam has been good and bad for the area.

Make a list of jobs that became available after the Aswan High Dam was built.

Research

You will need:
- encyclopedia (volume S)
- paper
- pencil

Read and report on important information about Anwar al-Sadat, the former Egyptian president. Share at least three interesting facts with your classmates.

Research

You will need:
- encyclopedia (volume D)
- paper
- pencil

Find the names and locations of the world's highest and largest dams. Compare these dams with the Aswan High Dam. Share your findings with the class.

Science

You will need:
- nonfiction information about the Nile River
- paper
- pencil

Describe at least four kinds of animal life that exist along the Nile River.

The Aswan High Dam and the Nile River

Here are some ways, good and bad, that the Aswan High Dam has affected the environment.

- controlled flooding
- supplied water for irrigation
- displaced people from their homes
- required farmers to use chemical fertilizers
- provided electrical power
- caused land erosion
- increased disease

Choose one issue and discuss its importance for the future of Egypt.

_____

_____

_____

_____

_____

_____

_____

_____

_____

_____

_____

_____

_____

_____

_____

The Sahara Desert

The Sahara Desert is the largest desert in the world covering 3.5 million square miles (5.5 million square km). It covers more than one-fourth of the continent of Africa and parts of ten different North African countries. The Sahara is one of the driest places in the world, averaging less than 2 inches (5 cm) of rainfall per year.

Much of the desert is covered with rocks and stony, flat plains. There are also many mountain ranges. Only about one-fifth of the desert is actually covered with sand. Temperatures can range from freezing (at night) to 122°F (50°C) in the heat of the day.

In this harsh **environment**, there are very few plants and animals. Animals must sleep during the day in underground holes to survive the heat. The **Sahara fox, desert scorpion, horned viper**, and **jerboa** are animals that have been able to adapt to life in the desert.

Native people move from one **oasis** to the next looking for water to survive. The Tuareg people of the Sahara are **nomads.** They raise a few crops as well as sheep and goats for meat and milk. Tuareg men cover their faces with veils and wear robes to the ground. They use camels for transportation because of the environment. The men enjoy racing the camels to test their **endurance** and **prowess** in handling the animals. The Tuareg people cross the desert in **caravans,** trading items like gold, pepper, **kola** nuts, and parrots, for goods that they need, such as cloth, metal, and rugs. They carry water in goatskin bags and make **portable** homes of woven grass and camel skin.

Answer in complete sentences:

1. Describe the area covered by the Sahara Desert.

2. Why is water necessary for survival?

3. What would daily life be like for a Tuareg child?

4. What items are traded by the Tuareg caravans?

5. What animals are native to the Sahara desert?

Web site:
i-cias.com/m.s/algeria/tamanra.htm

Creative Writing

You will need:

✔ paper
✔ pencil
✔ nonfiction materials about the Tuareg

What do you think Tuareg children do for pleasure? What kinds of toys might they have?

Science

You will need:

✔ nonfiction books about desert animals
✔ paper
✔ pencil

Research information about dromedary camels. Explain their importance to daily life in the desert. How have they adapted to the barren environment?

Research information about the hedgehog, fringe-toed lizard, lanner falcon, desert scorpion, horned viper, jerboa and Sahara fox—all animals that live in desert environments.

Math

You will need:

✔ calculator

The area of the Sahara Desert is three and a half million square miles (5.5 million square km).

The area of the continental United States is about three million square miles (4.8 million square km).

Determine the percentage of difference between the two. How much larger is the Sahara than the continental United States?

Social Studies

You will need:

✔ a map of the African continent
✔ a blank map
✔ paper
✔ pencil

List the ten North African countries that include some part of the Sahara Desert.

Locate and label the Hoggar Mountains and Tibesti Mountains.

The Sahara Desert

Circle the items in each group that are typical of life in the desert. Add one new item to each group.

food

couscous
goats' milk
potatoes
hot dogs

_____

transportation

camels
automobiles
airplane
wagon train

_____

climate/ environment

arid
hilly
barren
grassy

_____

clothing

sandals
dress
robes
suit and tie

_____

shelter

apartments
camel skin tents
brick house
trailer

_____

You are going on a week-long trek in the Sahara Desert. Decide which country or countries you will be traveling through. Will you need visas? shots? a guide? What kind of food and clothing will you need? What languages are spoken there? Create diary entries for each day of your trip.

Bonus
Something else to consider: What is the political situation in the country you are visiting? Describe some current events.

Serengeti National Park

Serengeti National Park is part of a 10,000-square mile (16,090 km) area known as the Serengeti **Ecosystem** in Tanzania. There are places in the park reserved for wildlife and areas where the Masai people use the land to graze their cattle. Serengeti National Park is about the size of Connecticut.

Every year in May a huge **migration** of **wildebeests** begins in the southern Serengeti. The animals move north to the Kenyan border, but many are lost crossing the Mara River. They graze for about two months at the Masai Mara National Reserve in Kenya which has a common **boundary** with Tanzania's Serengeti National Park. When the grass is gone, the wildebeests return to the Serengeti and wait for the next rainy season. During this time, the sky is often filled with tourists taking pictures from hot air balloons.

Many other wild animals live in the Serengeti, including giraffes, elephants, buffalo, lions, zebras, ostriches, and antelope. There are also many colorful and interesting species of birds.

Olduvai Gorge, located within the Serengeti, is not a place to view animals. Important discoveries about the **origin** of humans were made in this area by Mary and Louis Leakey in 1959. They uncovered bones of early **hominids** that are believed to be 600,000 years old.

Answer in complete sentences:

1. What discoveries were made at Olduvai Gorge?

2. What wild animals live in Serengeti National Park?

3. Through what two countries do the wildebeests migrate?

4. What African culture group grazes cattle in the Serengeti?

Web site:
www.gorp.com/thomson/serengeti.htm

Language Arts

You will need:
- ✔ stationery and envelope
- ✔ pen
- ✔ stamp

Write to the:

African Wildlife Foundation
1717 Massachusetts Avenue NW
Washington DC 20036

for information about safaris for people interested in wildlife conservation.

Creative Writing

You will need:
- ✔ lightweight tagboard cut to 4" x 6" (102 x 152 mm)
- ✔ pencil or pen,
- ✔ fine line markers

Design and write postcards to three of your friends telling about a recent visit to the Serengeti.

Social Studies

You will need:
- ✔ nonfiction information about animal conservation
- ✔ paper
- ✔ pencil

Make a list of illegal animal products in Africa and discuss items that could replace each one.

Find out about a conservation success story that is happening in Africa.

Art

You will need:
- ✔ paper
- ✔ pencil
- ✔ markers or crayons

Make a drawing of a safari jacket and suggest something that could be carried inside each pocket.

Serengeti National Park

The Masai use parts of the Serengeti to graze their cattle. Some Africans believe that the area should be used as farmland to help feed their people. Others feel that the area should be preserved for the wildlife. Which is more important, crops or wild animals?

Complete this chart:

Farmland

pros   cons

_____   _____

_____   _____

_____   _____

_____   _____

Wildlife Preservation

pros   cons

_____   _____

_____   _____

_____   _____

_____   _____

How do you think the Serengeti should be used? Explain.

_____

_____

Can you think of a way the two groups could agree?

_____

_____

_____

The Suez Canal

The Suez Canal in Egypt is about 100 miles (160 km) long and connects the Mediterranean and Red Seas through the Gulf of Suez. It is the shortest path for ships traveling between Europe and the Persian Gulf, Pakistan, Australia, India, and the Far East. The canal also provides the shortest water **route** for ships traveling from the east coast of North America to **ports** on the Indian Ocean.

In 1854, a Frenchman, Ferdinand De Lesseps, was given permission to dig the canal. Work began in 1859 and the canal was opened on November 17, 1869. Over the years, the canal has been made deeper and wider to **accommodate** larger ships.

Because it is an important **international** trade route, the Suez Canal must be kept open to all ships. In 1956, Egypt took control of the canal and fought off an unsuccessful **invasion** of the area by Israel, Britain, and France, countries that did not want Egypt to have control of the canal. During the 1967 war with Israel, the canal was closed.

Answer in complete sentences:

1. Who was Ferdinand De Lesseps?

2. How long did it take to build the canal?

3. Why has the canal been made deeper and wider over the years?

4. What country has control of the canal?

Web site:
pharos.bu.edu/Egypt/Wonders/Modern/suezcanal.html

Geography

You will need:
- ✔ map of the world
- ✔ pencil

Locate the Suez Canal on a map. Mark the water route between Europe and the East, and North America and the Indian Ocean.

Name five port cities a ship could pass traveling from the east coast of North America to ports on the Indian Ocean.

Social Studies

You will need:
- ✔ newspaper articles
- ✔ periodicals
- ✔ paper
- ✔ pencil

What is the current relationship between Israel and Egypt? Who are the leaders of each country? Why is it best for each country that the Suez Canal remain open?

Creative Writing

You will need:
- ✔ map of the world
- ✔ paper
- ✔ pencil

Find another place on the map where you think building a canal would be useful. Draw the new canal, name it, and write three ways the canal would help neighboring countries.

Science

You will need:
- ✔ encyclopedia (volume C)
- ✔ paper
- ✔ pencil

Compare and contrast the lock-and-lake canal system of the Panama Canal with the Suez Canal.

Compare the Suez Canal with the Panama Canal. Tell how the two canals are similar and different.

The Suez Canal

International Trade

The Suez Canal runs north from the Mediterranean Sea to the Red Sea in the south. Cargo ships travel through the canal each day. Use a map or globe to help you answer these questions.

Which way does each ship go? (circle one)

North	South	1. Oil from Saudi Arabia to Europe and the United States
North	South	2. Cars from Japan to Europe
North	South	3. Tools from Germany to India
North	South	4. Iron ore from Australia to England
North	South	5. Wine from France to Japan
North	South	6. Carpets from India to the Netherlands.
North	South	7. Cheese from Italy to Singapore
North	South	8. Toys from China to Spain
North	South	9. Salmon from Norway to Thailand
North	South	10. Wheat from the United States to Saudi Arabia

Answers:
1. North   2. North   3. South   4. North   5. South
6. North   7. South   8. North   9. South   10. South

Asia, Australia, New Zealand

Asia covers about one-third of the world's land area. It is the largest continent in both size and population. There are 49 countries on the continent, including China, the most populous nation in the world. India, another Asian country, has the second largest population.

The cities of Asia are very much like Western cities. They have high-rise apartments and office buildings, airports, theaters, television, shopping centers, and factories.

Australia lies in the South Pacific Ocean and the Indian Ocean. It is the only country that is also a continent. It is called the "land down under" because it lies in the Southern Hemisphere. Most of the people live in the two largest cities on the southeastern coast, Sydney and Melbourne. The rest of the continent is thinly populated.

The first people of Australia were Aborigines, most of whom live in rural areas. the majority of Australia's people came from England and Ireland.

Australia is famous for its unusual wildlife, including kangaroos, platypuses, koala, wombats, and tropical birds.

New Zealand is an island country. There are two main islands and several smaller ones. The country has a strong economy based on agriculture, manufacturing, and tourism.

New Zealand is a land of rivers, waterfalls, volcanoes, and evergreen forests. It has a mild, rainy climate. More than half of the land is given over to agriculture and pasture land. Tourism and manufacturing are growing and have become important sources of income for many people.

New Zealand's farmers produce enough meat and dairy products to feed its people and still have extra for export. The country has about 58 million sheep, raised for meat and wool, 8 million dairy and beef cattle, and 3,583,000 people.

Al-Haram and Mecca

Mecca is the holiest city of Islam. It is the birthplace of Muhammad, the Islamic **prophet**. Muslims around the world pray facing Mecca each day. Millions of Muslims travel to Mecca each year on a religious **pilgrimage** called *hajj*.

The city is in a hot, dry area of Saudi Arabia where there is little agriculture. The production of religious articles is the most important industry. Mecca also has a large income from feeding and housing more than two million pilgrims who come to the city each year.

No one who is not a Muslim is allowed inside Mecca. There is no violence to people, animals, or plants allowed inside the city. **Pilgrims** wear special clothing to be considered pure. Muslims declare their desire to obey Allah (God) by making the pilgrimage to Mecca.

The central place of worship in Mecca is Al-Haram, a **mosque** that was begun in the eighth century A.D. Over the centuries it has grown larger and more **ornate**. Al-Haram, the Great Mosque, can hold over 300,000 people. The first stop for the pilgrims is at Kaaba, in the center of the courtyard at Al-Haram. The Kaaba is a small building covered with a black curtain **embroidered** with verses from the Koran, the Muslim holy book. Each person walks seven times around the Kaaba and then touches or kisses the sacred Black Stone.

Answer in complete sentences:

1. What is the importance of Mecca to Muslims?

2. What is Al-Haram?

3. What ritual do Muslims follow at Kaaba?

4. How do people in Mecca earn a living?

5. What are some characteristics of Islamic religious architecture?

Web sites:

darkwing.uoregon.edu/~kbatarfi/makkah.html
darkwing.uoregon.edu/~kbatarfi/islam.html

Creative Writing

You will need:
- ✔ nonfiction information about Saudi Arabia and Islam
- ✔ paper
- ✔ pencil

What are the problems of managing the huge number of people coming to Mecca each year? Who is responsible for sanitation, drinking water, etc.?

Art

You will need:
- ✔ 12" x 18" (305 x 457 mm) construction paper
- ✔ scissors
- ✔ potato
- ✔ rule
- ✔ pictures of Islamic buildings and prayer rugs
- ✔ table knife
- ✔ ink pad
- ✔ pencil

Make an Islamic prayer mat! Cut the potato in half and draw a geometric design on it. Cut away the excess potato so the design is raised about ½" (13 mm). Use the scissors to fringe the two 12" (305 mm) sides of the paper. Use the ruler to measure a border inside the fringe. Press the potato stamp onto the ink pad and decorate the paper.

Research

You will need:
- ✔ nonfiction information about Saudi Arabia and Islam
- ✔ paper
- ✔ pencil

What events in Muhammad's life made him a prophet? What is his connection to Mecca?

Social Studies

You will need:
- ✔ nonfiction information about India, Hindus, Islam, and Mecca
- ✔ paper
- ✔ pencil

Explain what Hindus do on a pilgrimage to the Ganges River in Varanasi, India.

From what countries do people come to visit Mecca? What is their reason? How do they behave? dress?

Al-Haram and Mecca

Ninety-eight percent of people living in Saudi Arabia are Muslims. Their way of life is determined by their religion. How do you think life in Saudi Arabia would change if the people permitted foreign influences? Complete this chart with your ideas.

	Traditional	Foreign Influences
Government	The Koran is the constitution.	
Family	Marriages are arranged. Men may have four wives.	
Housing	All adults get a plot of land and a loan to build a house.	
Women's Rights	They may not drive cars. They must wear a black robe and cover their faces with a veil in public.	
Food	No alcohol or drugs are allowed. No pork may be eaten.	
Holidays	The Islamic holidays are based on the lunar calendar; the dates change each year.	
Fine Arts	Drawing humans or animals is not allowed for Islamic religious artworks. Music is not allowed in Islamic religious services.	

Angkor Wat

Angkor Wat is a temple that still stands in the ruins of Angkor, once the center of the Khmer Empire in Cambodia. Angkor means "city" and Wat means "temple" in the Khmer language. The city was abandoned when **invaders** from Siam (Thailand) conquered the **empire** in the 1400s. It was "discovered" in 1860 by the Western world when Henri Mouhot, a French **naturalist**, and his companions found the three-story building. The temple has five towers that are still standing and that are shaped like **lotus** blossoms.

Angkor Wat was built for King Suryavarman II during the 12th century. On his death it became his tomb. The temple was originally used for Hindu, then Buddhist, worship and was still in use by Buddhist monks when it was "discovered" by the Western world. The monks had taken care of the temple building and walls. The **corridors** of the temple were lined with artwork showing scenes from ancient **mythology**. Unfortunately, jungle **vegetation** had done a lot of damage to the other structures of the city.

After Mouhot's death, French historians and archaeologists continued to study the lost city. They worked for almost 100 years clearing paths, repairing buildings, and restoring monuments. Their work stopped for a time during the Civil War (1960–80). Unfortunately, soldiers damaged some of the **restoration**.

Answer in complete sentences:

1. What is Angkor Wat and who "discovered" it?

2. Describe Angkor Wat.

3. What efforts have been made to restore Angkor Wat?

4. How would a building in your community deteriorate if left unattended for many years?

Web site:
www.geocities.com/Times/Square/1848/angkor.html

Art

You will need:
- ✔ large white paper
- ✔ markers
- ✔ pictures of the corridor paintings of Angkor Wat

Explore the existing drawings in the Angkor Wat corridors. Add to them by creating your own versions with markers.

Social Studies

You will need:
- ✔ nonfiction books about world religion
- ✔ encyclopedia (volumes H and B)
- ✔ paper
- ✔ pencil

Make a list of the religious beliefs of Hinduism and Buddhism. What religious practices are common in Hindu and Buddhist homes?

Creative Writing

You will need:
- ✔ paper
- ✔ pencil

Describe what your life would have been like if you had been a Buddhist monk taking care of the ruins at Angkor Wat. Describe your daily life.

Science

You will need:
- ✔ nonfiction books about Cambodia
- ✔ encyclopedia (volume K)
- ✔ paper
- ✔ pencil

What are the weather conditions in the Cambodian jungle? What plants, animals, and insects are native? How do plants take over in the jungle? Why does this happen more in the tropics? What does it "feel like" to be exposed to tropical weather?

Angkor Wat

A Do-It-Yourself Jungle Expedition

Here is your chance to be a naturalist, archaeologist, or explorer. Complete the information about a real or make-believe expedition.

Where will you go? _____ How long will you stay? _____

What time of year? _____ How will you travel? _____

What shots will you need? _____

What will you pack? _____, _____, _____

_____, _____, _____

For what will you search? _____

For what problems might you prepare? _____

Draw a map of your destination.

Draw your most important discovery.
Describe it. What are its origin and value?

_____

_____

_____

_____

_____

Uluru (Ayers Rock)

Uluru (Ayers Rock), located in central Australia, rises 2,845 feet (867 m) above sea level and is an oval 2.2 miles (3.5 km) long and 1.5 miles (2.4 km) wide. It appears to change color (orange to red to purple) with the time of day. Uluru was called Ayers Rock after the former South Australian **premier**, Sir Henry Ayers. In 1977 Ayers Rock and the surrounding area were renamed Uluru and Uluru National Park. Uluru is an ancient Aborigine name for the rock.

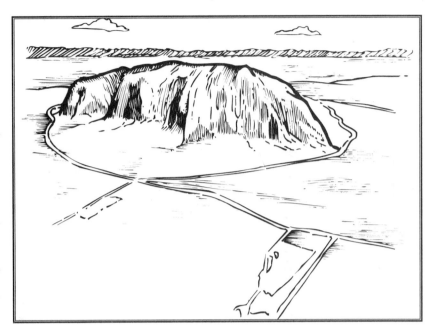

The **monolith**, made of **arkosic sandstone**, is a natural land formation. It is the most important tourist attraction in central Australia. Paintings in the **shallow** caves of Uluru are sacred to Aborigines and many depict their belief in *Dreamtime.* In 1958, official ownership of the rock was given to the Aborigines who have chosen to lease it back to the government for 99 years.

Scientists believe that the first Aborigines came to Australia from New Guinea about 40,000 years ago. They were hunter-gatherers who burnt down the forests to drive animals out and kill them. Aboriginal cave paintings tell stories of the earth's creation. Aborigines believe that nature and humans are part of each other. They worship the spirits of Dreamtime in holy places called *Dreaming Sites*. Their art, painted on rock walls, was part of their worship.

Answer in complete sentences:

1. What is Uluru and where is it located?

2. What are the Olga Mountains?

3. Who are the Aborigines?

4. Explain the Aboriginal belief in Dreamtime.

Web site:

www.about-australia.com/nt/ntatt.html

Science

You will need:
- map of the world
- pencil
- nonfiction books about geology, mountains, and rock formations

Read about other rock formations around the world like Monument Valley, Arizona/Utah, and Table Rock, South Africa. Locate and label them on a map.

Art

You will need:
- brown paper bag
- scissors
- markers

Cut the bag into an irregular shape and crumple it into a ball. Smooth it out and illustrate your idea of an Aboriginal drawing showing the creation of the earth.

Writing

You will need:
- nonfiction books about Australia and Aborigines
- paper
- pencil

Describe the culture and traditions of early Aborigines and explain how they have evolved over the years.

What is life like for Aborigines living in Australia today?

Geography

You will need:
- atlas
- colored pencils
- blank map of Australia

Create a topographical map showing as much information as possible about central Australia. Mark the Olga Mountains and Uluru.

Uluru (Ayers Rock)

Word Search Puzzle

```
I A C I D E I J E N A O R A N G E A
F I N R F M E D L I N E O P T H C Y
O E D A E N P S C E T L M H P A U E
L A P R Y A E U C I E U R H W Y P R
G I G H E V T C R V Y D H U F I E S
A H H D A A I I E P S V N N H R F R
M E C C P J M L O E L E S S U E E O
O D B U T A A T N N W E R T R N H C
U S D D L E I I I N O O A E O P C K
N A W N S U G N T M W N E T L O H E
T C T T R I R N T C E H S E G O G D
A R H I R H R U E I A D R T W H E C
I E E O O T D E M O N O L I T H O A
N D B R M D I D E A C G N H R A L T
S A H C E G I I S B Z M S R E N O O
R H A U S T R A L I A D H T T N G V
A F O R M A T I O N R D T I B N Y A
E E M Y H A N Y O O S D O C U E G L
```

Can you find these words?

ORANGE	PAINTINGS	OLGA MOUNTAINS
PURPLE	SACRED	CREATION
ULURU	DREAMTIME	AYERS ROCK
MONOLITH	ABORIGINES	OVAL
SANDSTONE	AUSTRALIA	SEA LEVEL
FORMATION	WORSHIP	NATURE
CAVES		GEOLOGY

The Dead Sea

The Dead Sea, located in Israel and Jordan, lies about 1,310 feet (399 meters) below sea level. It is the lowest and saltiest body of water in the world. It is called the Dead Sea because no fish (except brine shrimp) can live in its waters. Few plants grow in the salty soil around the sea. Swimmers can float easily in the salt water which is seven times saltier than the water in the oceans.

The Dead Sea gets water from several small streams and the Jordan River. The Dead Sea is 11 miles (18 kilometers) wide and about 50 miles (80 kilometers) long. The water level is slowly falling from lack of rain in the area and because the hot climate causes water to evaporate quickly.

The area around the Dead Sea holds many ancient treasures. It is believed that fragments of five cities from Biblical times are hidden under its waters. The Dead Sea Scrolls, the oldest manuscripts of the Bible, were found in 1947 by Bedouin shepherds searching for a lost goat in caves along the northwestern shore.

The scrolls, made of leather and papyrus, include the books of the Old Testament, psalms, and writings about the Qumran community. Other caves were searched in the 1950s and 1960s and more scrolls were found. They are believed to have been part of the library of a group of Jewish scholars who lived in the area about 150 B.C.

Answer in complete sentences:

1. Why is this body of water called the Dead Sea?

2. Who discovered the first Dead Sea Scrolls?

3. What are the Dead Sea Scrolls? Why are they important?

4. How much rainfall does the Dead Sea receive each year?

Web site:

sunsite.unc.edu/expo/deadsea.scrolls.html

Art

You will need:
- ✔ roll paper
- ✔ weak tea
- ✔ fine line marker
- ✔ rubber band

Crumple a length of paper and dip it in the tea. Allow it to dry in the sun so that it will look aged. Print a favorite poem on the scroll. Roll tightly and hold closed with the rubber band. Remove the band after a few hours.

Research

You will need:
- ✔ encyclopedia (volume B)
- ✔ paper
- ✔ pencil

Who are the Bedouins? Write five facts that interest you about their community and culture.

Social Studies

You will need:
- ✔ newspapers
- ✔ nonfiction information about Jerusalem
- ✔ paper
- ✔ pencil

The Dead Sea is 15 miles (24 km) east of Jerusalem and is part of the boundary between Israel and Jordan. What problems exist between the two countries today? In what ways do they agree?

Research

You will need:
- ✔ encyclopedia (volume D)
- ✔ paper
- ✔ pencil

What other minerals are found in the Dead Sea? What products are made from them?

The Dead Sea

Current Events Summary Form
(Middle East)

Date on the article _____

Headline _____

Countries/People _____   Glue the article here.

_____

_____

Problem _____

_____

_____

_____

Details _____

_____

_____

_____

Suggest a solution (if appropriate)

_____

_____

_____

_____

The Forbidden City

The Emperor Zhu Di planned the capital city of Peking (now known as Beijing), China. It was the center of the world to the ancient Chinese people. Chinese architects like to fit buildings into the **landscape**. Their designs were made of wood and marble. Most buildings had screen walls and were raised on **podiums** because of dampness. The roofs were tiled in golden yellow. Each building was positioned within the city walls according to its **status** and function.

The Forbidden City was a huge rectangle surrounded by a **moat** and a 35-foot-high (10.7 m) wall. Much of the original city was destroyed by fire and rebuilt in the 18th and 19th centuries. There are gates on the north and south ends.

The city was built in three main parts. Houses, shops, and government buildings were around the outside of the city. The middle section was a beautiful area of lakes and gardens and in the center was the **Imperial** palace. This was an area just for the emperor, his family, court, and people doing government business. The emperor lived in luxury and **seclusion**. Ordinary people could not enter the Forbidden City.

The palace complex contained about 1,000 buildings. The most important building was the Hall of Supreme Harmony. This was where the emperor and his court gathered for state celebrations. In 1949, the Forbidden City was restored and opened to the public as the Palace Museum.

Answer in complete sentences:

1. Explain what you read about Chinese architecture.

2. Describe the planning and positioning of buildings within the Forbidden City.

3. How would your life be different if you were confined within the city walls?

4. When was the Forbidden City restored as a museum?

Web site:
pasture.ecn.purdue.edu/~agenhtml/agenmc/china/scenfc.htm

Art

You will need:

✔ nonfiction books about Chinese mythology
✔ art supplies

Learn about the dragon in Chinese mythology. Design a dragon, cut out the shape, and glue it to background paper.

Science

You will need:

✔ nonfiction books about gardening
✔ art supplies

Learn about the design of an Asian garden. Make drawings of several flowers or the layout a garden.

Research

You will need:

✔ nonfiction books about styles of architecture around the world
✔ art supplies

Choose one style of architecture that appeals to you. (Do not choose Chinese). Compare and contrast your choice with the buildings inside the Forbidden City.

Social Studies

You will need:

✔ encyclopedia (volume C)
✔ other related nonfiction books
✔ paper
✔ pencil

How did life in China change when the Communists came to power in 1949? Explain the government and politics of China today.

The Forbidden City

The last emperor of China was Pu Yi. He came to the throne at the age of two (1908). Pu Yi seldom left the Forbidden City until 1924 when he was forced out by the changing Chinese political climate.

Use what you know about the Forbidden City and the Imperial Palace to reconstruct a day in the life of the young Pu Yi. Here are some suggestions to help you get started:

- Tutors schooled him in the English language and Western ways.

- He was occupied by the pageantry of "playing" emperor.

- He was surrounded by servants who often carried him on a palanquin.

- In 1922, he was married to Wan Jung.

- He introduced bicycles, telephones, movies, Western clothes, and magazines to the Imperial Palace.

- He admittedly did not know the value of money.

- At the end of his reign, the Imperial Household was bankrupt.

Do you think he had a happy childhood? Explain.

_____

_____

_____

_____

_____

_____

_____

_____

_____

_____

_____

_____

_____

_____

_____

The Grand Palace

The Grand Palace in Bangkok, Thailand, includes several palaces and temples built over a period of 200 years. The **Emerald** Buddha, Thailand's most precious **shrine**, can be seen in the Wat Phra Kaeo, a temple on the Palace grounds. The Grand Palace is the home of Thailand's royalty and is used for banquets and receiving foreign **dignitaries**.

The *bot* is the largest original structure at the temple of Wat Phra Kaeo. It holds the Emerald Buddha on a 30-foot-high (9.1 m) **pedestal**. The statue, made of **jade**, is about 30 inches (76.2 cm) tall. The people of Thailand believe that as long as the Emerald Buddha is in their country, Thailand will be free. Each season of the year, a ceremony is held and the king changes the costume on the Emerald Buddha. No one may take pictures of the Emerald Buddha.

The palace grounds are landscaped with beautifully shaped trees and plants. There are memorials and statues of great value and importance to the Thai people. The outdoor murals of the Ramayana picture the ancient story of the triumph of good over evil. Thai artists have painted the original story in 178 panels that are close to a mile (1.6 km) in length.

A beautiful Chinese gate decorated with **porcelain** tiles greets visitors to the palace buildings. Behind the gate is the Phra Maha Monthien, home of early kings. Only the main hall of the **complex**, which holds a traditional *busbok* (an open-sided throne with a spired roof), is open to the public.

One of the finest buildings on the grounds is the Chakri Maha Prasad, built in the European style with three Thai **spires**. It houses **reception** rooms and a throne room where the king receives foreign **ambassadors**. Inside another building is the Audience Hall of Amarin, the **coronation** room used for important royal ceremonies.

Answer in complete sentences:

1. What buildings are on the grounds of the Grand Palace?

2. What royal ceremonies and activities take place in each building?

3. Describe the Emerald Buddha. Where is it housed?

4. Why is the Emerald Buddha special to the Thai people?

Web site:
www.cs.ait.ac.th/~wutt/wutt.html

Social Studies

You will need:
- ✔ nonfiction information about Thailand
- ✔ Thai cookbook
- ✔ paper
- ✔ pencil

Plan refreshments for dignitaries visiting the Grand Palace.
Include a recipe for one food item.

Art

You will need:
- ✔ drawing paper
- ✔ markers
- ✔ pencil
- ✔ pictures of Buddhas

Even though no pictures are taken of the Emerald Buddha, find pictures of another Buddha.

Design costumes for the Emerald Buddha to wear in the hot, cool, and rainy seasons.

Research

You will need:
- ✔ encyclopedia (volume B)
- ✔ paper
- ✔ pencil

What are the main beliefs of Buddhism?

Who was Siddharta?

Make a list of five other Buddhist countries.

Geography

You will need:
- ✔ map of Asia
- ✔ atlas
- ✔ pen
- ✔ pencil

Locate Bangkok, Thailand, on the map. What is its latitude and longitude? What is the population of the country? What percentage of the people are Buddhist?

The Grand Palace

Fill in the missing words to complete the sentences.
The letters in the circles will spell a word to answer the last question.

1. The Emerald Buddha sits on a high _____ .

2. The Emerald _____ may not be photographed.

3. A beautiful Chinese _____ greets palace visitors.

4. Thailand is ruled by a _____ .

5. The Grand _____ is the home of Thailand's royalty.

6. The _____ of Ramayana picture the story of good over evil.

7. The busbok is a traditional _____ with a spired roof.

8. The Emerald Buddha is made of _____ .

1. __ __ __ __ __ ◯ __ __

2. __ __ __ __ ◯ __

3. __ ◯ __ __

4. __ ◯ __ __

5. __ __ ◯ __ __ __

6. __ __ __ ◯ __ __

7. __ __ __ __ ◯ __

8. __ __ ◯ __

In what country is the Grand Palace? __ __ __ __ __ __ __ __

Answers:
1. pedestal   2. Buddha   3. gate   4. king   5. Palace
6. murals   7. throne   8. jade.
THAILAND

The Great Barrier Reef

The Great **Barrier Reef** is in the Coral Sea. It stretches along the coast of Australia for about 1,250 miles or 2,011 kilometers. This group of coral separates the shallow coastal waters from the open sea. The reef is the largest structure ever built by living creatures. It contains more than 400 **species** of **coral polyps**.

During its lifetime, the coral polyp enlarges its skeleton with **secretions** of lime. The polyps live together in colonies. When one dies, a new one arrives to live on top of the skeleton. Polyps are always growing and changing in the deep blue and **emerald** sea around the Great Barrier Reef. Tiny plants called **algae** give coral much of their color. They also provide food for it. These plants are found in shallow water because they need sunlight to live and grow.

The Great Barrier Reef is home to many unusual fish and **marine** animals. It attracts thousands of tourists each year who enjoy diving, fishing, and swimming in the clear, blue **lagoons**. Tourists also take guided trips through the area in glass-bottomed boats. A park has been established to protect the coral reef.

The balance of nature at the reef can be upset very easily. In the 1980s large sections of the reef were eaten by crown-of-thorns starfish. Additional damage was done by people who broke off coral for souvenirs. It will take many years for the reef to recover.

Answer in complete sentences:

1. Explain the life cycle of a coral polyp.

2. What might a visitor to the Great Barrier Reef see and do?

3. How has the balance of nature been threatened at the reef?

4. What might marine biologists do to protect the reef from damage?

Web sites:

www.lonelyplanet.com/dest/aust/gbreef.htm

www.about-australia.com/qld/qldatt.htm

Social Studies

You will need:
- ✔ nonfiction books about Australia
- ✔ map
- ✔ pencil
- ✔ colored pencils
- ✔ grid paper

Trace the map of Australia. Create a legend for your map. Color the length of the Great Barrier Reef.

Science

You will need:
- ✔ nonfiction books about careers in science
- ✔ paper
- ✔ pencil

Learn more about marine biology as a career. Determine what training is necessary and write a brief job description.

Research

You will need:
- ✔ nonfiction books about water pollution and marine environments
- ✔ paper
- ✔ pencil

Learn more about human/environmental relationships and their consequences. Discuss the importance of safe water for the world's survival. How does water pollution impact you and your family?

Science

You will need:
- ✔ nonfiction book about marine creatures and their environment
- ✔ drawing paper
- ✔ markers
- ✔ pencil

Draw and label a diagram showing a cross section of a coral polyp. Make a list and drawings of several species of coral. Make a list and drawings of several species of fish living in the Pacific Ocean. Contact your local zoo or aquarium to see which of those fish are on display.

The Great Barrier Reef

Read the information and label the pictures.

This sea snail feeds on the crown-of-thorns starfish: **triton**
This sea creature destroys coral polyps: **crown-of-thorns starfish**
These animals form a reef in shallow water: **coral**
This predator feeds on small fish: **white-tipped reef shark**
These marine reptiles can swim up to 20 miles (32.2 km) per hour: **sea turtles**
This mollusk uses suction cups on 10 arms to catch prey: **squid**

The Great Wall of China

The Great Wall of China, begun in the third century B.C., is the most **extensive** building project ever undertaken by the human race. It is the only structure manufactured by humans that can be seen from the moon. The most popular section for tourists to visit is at Badaling, north of Beijing.

Made of earth, stone, and brick, the 1,500-mile-wall (2,400 km) across the northern boundary was built primarily by Shih-Huang-Ti, the First Supreme **Emperor** of China. It was meant to keep out nomadic people who threatened to **raid** his country.

The Emperor ordered his soldiers to force every able-bodied person (about one million men) to work repairing and connecting existing walls. Groups of workers shaped dirt into high **mounds.** Others made bricks from clay. Some cut large, square stones. The bricks and stones were then fitted onto the sides of the earth mounds. **Watchtowers** were built every 100 yards (91.4 m) along the length of the wall. Roadways were built on the top. The finished project, which took ten years to complete, was ten people wide and five people high.

Shih-Huang-Ti had come up with a brilliant solution. The nomads were not able to raid China with so many soldiers and workers on the wall. Over the years, many emperors made improvements to the wall, but today some of the sections lie in ruins. Portions of the Great Wall have been rebuilt by the People's Republic of China.

Answer in complete sentences:

1. Who was Shih-Huang-Ti and what did he do?

2. How was the Great Wall built?

3. Explain what we know about the size of the Great Wall.

4. What kind of machinery and tools would be used to build the Great Wall in modern times?

Web site:
www.net.edu.cn/beijing/GreatWall.html

Math

You will need:

✔ paper
✔ pencil

Estimate the dimensions of a wall that is ten people wide and five people high.

Science

You will need:

✔ paper
✔ pencil

The Chinese invented the wheelbarrow to make their work go faster. For what was it probably used? Make a list of other labor-saving devices that do not require electricity.

Creative Writing

You will need:

✔ paper
✔ pencil
✔ stapler
✔ markers
✔ construction paper cover

Make a small book and write the diary of a worker on the wall. Try to convey the details of difficulties and dangers they faced as they worked.

Social Studies

You will need:

✔ current information about the People's Republic of China
✔ paper
✔ pencil

How do you think current conditions and politics in China will affect rebuilding and repair of the Great Wall?

The Great Wall of China

Use a calculator to find the answer. What does the answer have to do with the Great Wall of China?

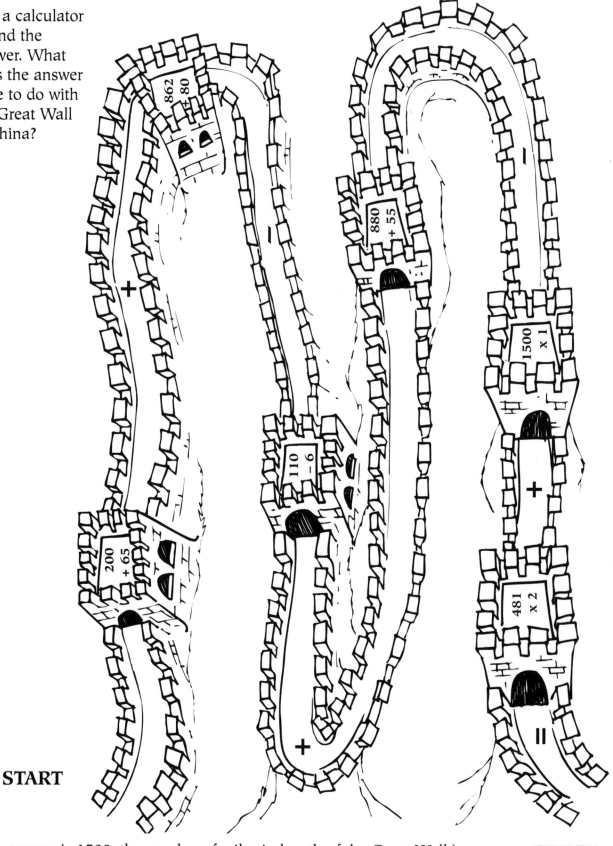

862 + 80

880 + 55

1500 × 1

200 + 65

110 − 6

481 × 2

START

FINISH

(The answer is 1500, the number of miles in length of the Great Wall.)

Healesville Wildlife Sanctuary

The Healesville Wildlife **Sanctuary** was opened in 1934 by a group of local people who gave their time and money to care for the **flora** and **fauna** in the area. Today this zoo, east of Melbourne, Australia, is a protected natural **environment** for native animals, birds, and plant life. More than 250,000 people visit each year.

It is a special place because the exhibits are built to allow visitors to move freely among the animals. Walkways in the **koala** exhibit are above ground level so that people can get a better look at these animals who stay in the treetops. There are **enclosed** exhibits for **nocturnal** animals and reptiles. In the 1940s, the Healesville Wildlife Sanctuary became the first zoo to breed a **platypus** in **captivity**. Today, the sanctuary has the best platypus exhibit in the world.

Natural areas are home to insects, reptiles, and small animals. A visitor may pass a **bearded dragon** sitting on a fence or a **skink** chasing flies. These reptiles are not dangerous as long as people do not frighten them.

Kangaroos walk freely on the grounds under the tall manna gum trees that grow in the sanctuary. Insects and spiders hide in the tree bark, tropical birds build nests, and koalas and **possums** sleep in branches. Termites chew the trees' dead wood. The trees and plants are an important part of the life cycle in the sanctuary.

As in every zoo, a crew of keepers feeds, cleans, and cares for the animals. Veterinarians watch over the animals' health needs, and a group of scientists works to protect the environment.

Answer in complete sentences:

1. What can a visitor see at the Healesville Wildlife Sanctuary?

2. Name four native Australian animals.

3. Where do the koalas live? What do they eat?

4. How do the manna gum trees provide a habitat for sanctuary animals?

Web site:
www.zoo.org.au/hs/hshome.htm

Language Arts

You will need:
- nonfiction information about Australian animals and birds
- paper
- pencil

Make a list of at least 20 native Australian animals in alphabetical order.

Geography

You will need:
- map of the world
- atlas
- paper
- pencil

Locate Melbourne, Australia, on a map of the world. List five other important Australian cities. Use the atlas to find the population of each city.

Creative Writing

You will need:
- nonfiction information about Australian animals
- paper
- pencil

Choose an animal and write a story about its best or worst day at Healesville Sanctuary. Tell three events and explain how each event affected the animal.

Animal list: wombat, echidna, koala, wallaby, kangaroo, emu, platypus, python, blue-tongued lizard, dingo, bettong, Tasmanian devil

Science

You will need:
- nonfiction information about Australian animals
- paper
- pencil

Choose one animal native to Australia. Make a drawing and chart information about its habitat and feeding. Be sure to indicate any unusual characteristics and explain how it has adapted to its surroundings.

Healesville Wildlife Sanctuary

Australia's Animals

Identify this animal and color it appropriately. Use a field guide if necessary.

The Imperial Palace

The Imperial Palace in Tokyo, Japan, is the home of the emperor and his family. It was built in the time of the **shoguns** and originally had three **moats** and 24 **drawbridges**. The palace sits high on a hill in the center of Tokyo. It is surrounded by a wall 50-feet (15.2 m) high with a locked gate. The emperor and his family live in a modern house that was built in 1970 on the palace grounds.

People are permitted to visit the palace only two days of each year, New Year's Day and the emperor's birthday. On those days, thousands of Japanese citizens gather to listen to the emperor's greeting.

The National Diet Building, home of Japan's **legislature,** is south of the palace. The palace was damaged by the Kanto earthquake and required extensive repairs in 1923.

The palace grounds cover 264 acres. The Imperial Palace East Garden was opened to the public in 1968. It includes a formal garden, private pond, and woods that separate the palace from the busy city. The **estate** is an important natural space in the heart of Tokyo.

Answer in complete sentences:

1. Where is the Imperial Palace? Who lives there?

2. When do people visit the palace?

3. Describe the grounds surrounding the palace.

4. What is the National Diet Building?

Web site:
www.city.net/countries/japan/tokyo

Creative Writing

You will need:

- ✔ paper
- ✔ pencil

What do you think the emperor says to the citizens in his greeting?

Why do you think people are only allowed inside the Imperial Palace for two days each year?

Do you think you would enjoy living inside the palace walls? Explain.

Social Studies/Art

You will need:

- ✔ tourist information about Tokyo
- ✔ paper
- ✔ pencil
- ✔ markers

Design a poster showing the Imperial Palace and at least one other Tokyo landmark.

Language Arts

You will need:

- ✔ paper
- ✔ dictionary
- ✔ pencil

Write sentences using two adjectives to describe each of these words: estate, drawbridge, emperor, shogun, moat.

Science

You will need:

- ✔ nonfiction information about gardens
- ✔ paper
- ✔ colored pencils

Design a traditional Japanese garden. Make a list of plants that would grow well in Japan's climate and explain their care.

Is there a formal garden or park near you? Visit and describe what you see. How does the area change with the seasons?

The Imperial Palace

Design a birthday greeting to the emperor for the Congratulations Register at the Imperial Palace. If you wish, include a small drawing in the Japanese style.

Kansai Airport

Kansai International Airport, 3 miles (4.8 km) off the coast of Honshu in Osaka Bay, Japan, was completed in 1994. The **terminal** building is on a **synthetic** island that took five years to build. The island is connected to the **mainland** by a bridge and railroad lines.

Creating a new island was a difficult job. First, engineers piled sand and earth 66 feet (20 m) deep in the seabed. Tons of crushed rock were dumped on top of that. Eventually, the weight of the rock squeezed out the water and made a solid foundation. Finally, a large steel frame was created to mark the **boundaries** of the island. The resulting island was 2.5 miles (4 km) long and .8 miles (1.3 km) wide.

The airport terminal building was designed by Renzo Piano, an Italian architect. The main part of the terminal is four stories high and is shaped like a huge airplane wing. There are 900 **columns** holding up the roof so that the height can be adjusted when necessary. (The island will be settling for several years.) The new airport has only one runway, operating 24 hours a day and serving 25 million passengers each year.

Answer in complete sentences:

1. Describe how the synthetic island was built.

2. Describe the terminal building.

3. How is the airport connected to the mainland?

4. Why do you think it is necessary for the airport to operate 24 hours a day?

Web site:
kiisnet.kiis.or.ip/kixinfo/kix.html

Research/Creative Writing

You will need:

✓ nonfiction information about airports
✓ paper
✓ pencil

Compare and contrast Kansai Airport with another large airport.

Write a story about the international airport nearest your home. Answer these questions:
- To what countries can you fly direct?
- How many international flights are there per week?

Math

You will need:

✓ calculator
✓ paper
✓ pencil

Compute the average number of people who use the Kansai Airport each month, week, day, and hour, based on 25 million passengers per year.

Art

You will need:

✓ paper
✓ book about making model planes

Read and follow directions for making several different paper planes. Fly them and try to determine which design is the best.

Science

You will need:

✓ nonfiction books about environmental pollution
✓ paper
✓ pencil

Learn more about noise pollution and how it affects people living near airports. List five ideas to improve the situation.

Kansai Airport

Arrival
(From)

City	Flight no.	Time	Gate
Beijing	128	2:45	16
Brussels	95	6:30	14
Copenhagen	67	1:10	18
Lisbon	144	3:20	13
Paris	183	4:15	15

Departure
(To)

City	Flight no.	Time	Gate
Athens	63	3:25	22
Bangkok	125	9:30	22
Frankfurt	97	10:10	25
Milan	117	4:15	24
Tel Aviv	55	6:45	26

Write five questions that can be answered using information from this chart. Pass your questions to a partner to answer.

1. _____

2. _____

3. _____

4. _____

5. _____

Example: At what gate and at what time will you meet your grandmother when she returns from her vacation in Paris? (Gate 15 at 4:15)

Lake Baikal

Lake Baikal is located in the Irkutsk region of Russia in southern **Siberia**. It is the world's deepest freshwater **lake**, as large as the country of Belgium and more than one mile (1.6 km) deep. Lake Baikal contains more water than all five of the Great Lakes of North America put together. It is known as "the Pearl of Siberia."

The lake is usually frozen from January to May. In summer it is warm enough for swimming. There is a hot springs nearby that is popular with tourists.

The **region** is home to 1,200 species of plants and animals found nowhere else in the world. Some of the most unusual are the Baikal seal, **sandhopper**, and a fish that gives birth to live young.

Today, the **environment** of Lake Baikal is **threatened** by factories that are dumping **chemicals** into the water. The Russian government is working with paper mills and factories to limit the amount of waste running into the lake. They have stopped building new factories on the **lakeshore** and may tear down some of the existing factories. The **community** wants to keep the environment and waters of Lake Baikal pure for the future.

Answer in complete sentences:

1. Where is Lake Baikal?

2. During what months is the lake frozen?

3. How is the lake environment being threatened?

4. How is the lake valuable to the community?

5. What animals live near the lake?

Web sites:
ripley.ece.uiuc.edu/~fridman/baikal.html
www.friends-partners.org/~irkutsk/fed/baikal.html

Language Arts

You will need:
- graph paper
- pencil

Design a word search puzzle using the vocabulary words. Ask your teacher to duplicate it for use in the center.

Choose and complete a word search puzzle made by one of your classmates.

Science

You will need:
- nonfiction information about Siberia
- graph paper
- pencil

Make a chart to show the seasons and average temperatures in Siberia for one year.

Creative Writing

You will need:
- paper
- pencil

Write a news article about a factory that is polluting Lake Baikal. Suggest a solution to the problem.

Design a travel brochure for a hot springs resort near Lake Baikal.

Geography

You will need:
- world map
- paper
- pencil
- calculator

Estimate how many miles and kilometers it is from your house to Lake Baikal. Trace a route on the map by air, land, and water.

Lake Baikal

Every community has a government. There may be a city manager or a mayor or a group of elected council members. These people must decide what is best for the community and make laws to protect the best interest of its citizens.

Answer these questions as if you were a member of a town council.

How is Lake Baikal valuable to your community?

1. _____

2. _____

3. _____

What would be your greatest concerns for Lake Baikal?

1. _____

2. _____

3. _____

What laws could be written to protect the environment around Lake Baikal?

1. _____

2. _____

3. _____

Make a plan for gaining cooperation from citizens and business leaders.

1. _____

2. _____

3. _____

Mount Everest

Mount Everest is the highest mountain in the world and part of the Himalayan mountain **range** which spans the border between India and China. Mount Everest lies between the small **kingdom** of Nepal and the province of Tibet. George Everest, a British surveyor general of India, led an **expedition** to map the Himalayas in 1856. The highest mountain in the range is a little more than 29,000 feet (8,839 m) and is named after him.

Mountain ranges are created when **currents** of **molten** rock beneath the earth's surface cause the plates of the earth's hard outer crust to smash together. The edges of the plates push together with such force that they are slowly pushed upward to make mountains. Mount Everest is still being pushed up. It gets about two inches higher (5 cm) each year.

In 1953, the first people reached the **summit** of Mount Everest. They were Edmund Hillary, a New Zealander, and Tenzing Nogay, a Sherpa mountaineer. Since that time, many climbers have successfully conquered the peak. In 1992, 32 climbers from 5 different expeditions reached the summit on the same day.

_____

Answer in complete sentences:

1. Explain how mountains are formed.

2. Who is George Everest and why is the mountain named after him?

3. Who were the first people to climb to the top of Mount Everest?

4. How do you imagine it would feel to climb to the summit of Mount Everest?

_____

Web site:
www.pscs.org/~syaap/everest.html

Research

You will need
- ✔ nonfiction books about mountain climbing and the Himalaya Mountains
- ✔ paper
- ✔ pencil

Make a list of mountain climbing gear appropriate for a Himalayan expedition.

What kind of training should one have before embarking on such a journey? What health considerations are there?

Science

You will need:
- ✔ nonfiction books about the Himalaya Mountains
- ✔ paper
- ✔ pencil

Read about the native animals of the area (ibex, yak, etc.). Choose one animal and write a paragraph about it. Make a drawing of the animal. Explain how the animal has adapted to life in the mountains.

Science

You will need:
- ✔ nonfiction books about geology
- ✔ art supplies

Read about how mountains are born. Make a model or a drawing to show what you learned.

Social Studies

You will need:
- ✔ nonfiction books about Nepal and Tibet
- ✔ paper
- ✔ pencil
- ✔ art supplies

Make drawings showing the the people of Nepal and Tibet and their homes. How does the mountain range affect their way of life?

Mount Everest

Help the mountaineer climb Mount Everest.

Shwe Dagon Pagoda

The Shwe Dagon **pagoda** in Rangoon, Burma, is a famous example of religious architecture. There is a huge *stupa,* a bell-shaped, gold-leafed monument in the center of the temple. The top of the *stupa* is covered with precious jewels. There are silver and gold bells on the *stupa* that ring softly when breezes blow. Sixty-four smaller *stupas* surround the main one. The landmark is valued at about $750 million.

There are many **temples** and pagodas in Burma. Each one has a legend about the **relics** it holds. Tradition says that Buddha gave Burmese travelers eight hairs to be **enshrined** in the Shwe Dagon pagoda. Four of the hairs were stolen by pirates. The remaining four hairs were brought to the king of Burma. When the king opened the box he was surprised to find all eight hairs. The hairs were giving off a bright light which seemed to heal blind, deaf, and crippled people. At the same time the box was opened, there was an earthquake, a thunderstorm, jewels fell from the sky, and all the trees **bore** fruit.

Answer in complete sentences:

1. What relics are stored inside the Shwe Dagon pagoda?

2. What makes the pagoda so valuable?

3. What must a pagoda have to give it religious importance?

4. Explain the legend of Shwe Dagon pagoda.

Web sites:
www.spyglass.com/~davet/travel/pictures/burma/shwedagon1.m.html
www.asiatour.com/myanmar/e-03yang/em-yan12.htm

Social Studies

You will need:
- ✔ nonfiction information about Burma
- ✔ paper
- ✔ pencil

In what ways have the Burmese blended their religion and traditional culture (theater, arts and crafts)?

Research

You will need:
- ✔ nonfiction information about pagodas and Burma
- ✔ paper
- ✔ pencil

What is a *nat* (or *chinthe*)? What is their purpose at a pagoda?

Make a list of ten other Burmese pagodas.

Creative Writing

You will need:
- ✔ paper
- ✔ pencil

Write a news story about the opening of the box containing eight hairs. Retell what happened and explain its importance to the people of Burma.

Interview the king and ask his feelings about the miracle of Buddha's hairs.

Art

You will need:
- ✔ drawing paper
- ✔ colored pencils
- ✔ pictures of Buddha

Make a drawing of a Buddha that might be inside a Burmese pagoda.

Shwe Dragon Pagoda

Directions: Write an original legend for your pagoda. What relics are inside? How did they get there? Decorate the outside.

Sydney Opera House

An international competition was held to design an opera house at Sydney, Australia. Jørn Utzon's innovative design won the contest. Work began on the **foundation** in 1959, but Utzon resigned the project after six years because of problems with the building crew. The Sydney Opera House was finished by a team of Australian architects.

It is located on Bennelong Point, a **peninsula** which allows the building to be viewed from all **angles**. The **profile** of its overlapping roofs look like a yacht coming into the harbor. The project took 14 years to complete. It is an art center meant for more than just opera performances.

The shell-shaped roofs are what makes the building special. Each of the shells was pre-made on the job site. They curve inward and are joined to each other by concrete. The shells are covered with white and **buff ceramic** tiles made in Sweden. The tiles are less than 5 inches (13 cm) square so that they can cover the curved surfaces. Special glass underneath the roofs has two layers that protect from the sun and block out the sounds of passing ships.

The Sydney Opera House was opened by Queen Elizabeth II in October 1973. There are four main halls: Opera Theater, Concert Hall, Playhouse, and Drama Theater, as well as a library, exhibition hall, and two restaurants. The Concert Hall, which seats more than 2,000 people, is designed with perfect acoustics for classical music. It houses the Grand Organ which is the largest mechanical organ in the world.

Answer in complete sentences:

1. Describe the appearance of the Sydney Opera House.

2. Who was the architect of the Sydney Opera House?

3. What facilities are located inside the Sydney Opera House?

4. Why would effective insulation be important at the Sydney Opera House? (Consider the location of the building.)

Web sites:
www.city.net/countries/australia/sydney
www.anzac.com/aust/nsw/soh.htm

Geography

You will need:
- ✓ world map
- ✓ paper
- ✓ pencil
- ✓ calculator

Estimate how many miles or kilometers it is from your house to the Sydney Opera House. Trace a route on the map by air, land, and water.

Social Studies

You will need:
- ✓ nonfiction information about Sydney, Australia
- ✓ map of Australia
- ✓ paper
- ✓ pencil

Locate Sydney, Australia, on the map. What products are exports and imports?

What types of boats use the harbor? How important is recreational boating?

Language Arts

You will need:
- ✓ paper
- ✓ pencil
- ✓ sample newspaper articles

Write an article describing the opening of an imaginary concert hall. Create your idea of a perfect concert program for the opening.

Creative Arts

You will need:
- ✓ nonfiction information about the Australian people
- ✓ paper
- ✓ pencil

Make a list of Australians involved in the arts. Classify them as painters, musicians, writers, actors, etc.

Sydney Opera House

Each of these compositions might be performed in the Sydney Opera House. Follow the directions.

Circle the opera titles. (There are three).

Underline the ballets. (There are three).

1. Peter and the Wolf

2. The Marriage of Figaro

3. Swan Lake

4. Don Giovanni

5. The Messiah

6. Rodeo

7. Madame Butterfly

8. Four Seasons

9. Water Music

10. The Nutcracker Suite

Which four titles are not marked?

_____

_____

_____

_____

Bonus: List five plays that might be performed in the playhouse or drama theater at the Sydney Opera House.

1. _____

2. _____

3. _____

4. _____

5. _____

(Numbers 2, 4, and 7 are operas, Numbers 3, 6, and 10 are ballets)

The Taj Mahal

The Taj Mahal is located on the banks of the Yamuna River in Agra, India. It is the burial **tomb** of Mumtaz Mahal, the favorite wife of Emperor Shah Jahan. It was begun in 1631. The **mausoleum** is believed to be one of the most perfect buildings in the world. It is **symmetric**, with each side being the same as the other. There is a reflecting pool on two sides of the monument. It is surrounded by beautiful gardens. The name, Taj Mahal, means "Crown of the Palace." The architect is unknown, but it is believed that the design included many of the Shah's own ideas and expressed his deep love for his wife.

The building has many characteristics of traditional Islamic architecture. It is raised above ground level on a red sandstone base called a **plinth**. The pointed **arches** are a symbol of the Muslim faith. Because the Shah loved jewels, he had the Taj Mahal decorated with **semi-precious** stones in flower patterns. The domed roof means there is a tomb below. It is the traditional Islamic symbol of **paradise**. High towers, called **minarets**, were used to call people to prayer five times a day. The arches are framed with writings from the **Koran**, the holy book of Islam, done in **calligraphy**. Under the large dome is an **octagonal** room which holds the remains of Mumtaz Mahal and Shah Jahan.

It took about 20 years for over 20,000 workers to complete the Taj Mahal. Today, visitors to the central chamber of the mausoleum see marble monuments called **cenotaphs** surrounded by beautifully carved and jeweled marble screens. They do not see the real tombs which are protected from vandals in an underground **crypt**.

Answer in complete sentences:

1. What is the meaning of the name Taj Mahal?

2. Explain three characteristics of traditional Islamic architecture.

3. What general statements can you make about Emperor Shah Jahan, his personal feelings, religious beliefs, interests, and wealth?

4. What does a visitor see in the central chamber of the mausoleum?

Web sites:
www.k.dmdr.demon.co.uk/taj.htm
www.meadev.gov.in/tourism/forts/taj.htm

Research

You will need:
- ✔ nonfiction books about gems
- ✔ a sheet of large chart paper

Locate and add information about a variety of semiprecious stones to the chart.

Art

You will need:
- ✔ book on calligraphy
- ✔ fine black markers

Practice calligraphy by writing your name or a familiar saying.

Math

You will need:
- ✔ a supply of 8 ½" (22 cm) square papers
- ✔ ruler
- ✔ pencil
- ✔ scissors
- ✔ chart showing a variety of symmetrical shapes

Choose several of the shapes to copy or design one of your own. Decorate them with flower patterns.

Social Studies

You will need:
- ✔ encyclopedia (volumes I and M)
- ✔ world map

Make a list of beliefs and practices of the Muslim religion. In what countries is it the main religion? Locate those countries on a map.

The Taj Mahal

In symmetry, both sides of an object are the same.

Try this: Fold a piece of scrap paper in half through the center.
Cut out a shape without cutting through the fold.
Open the paper.

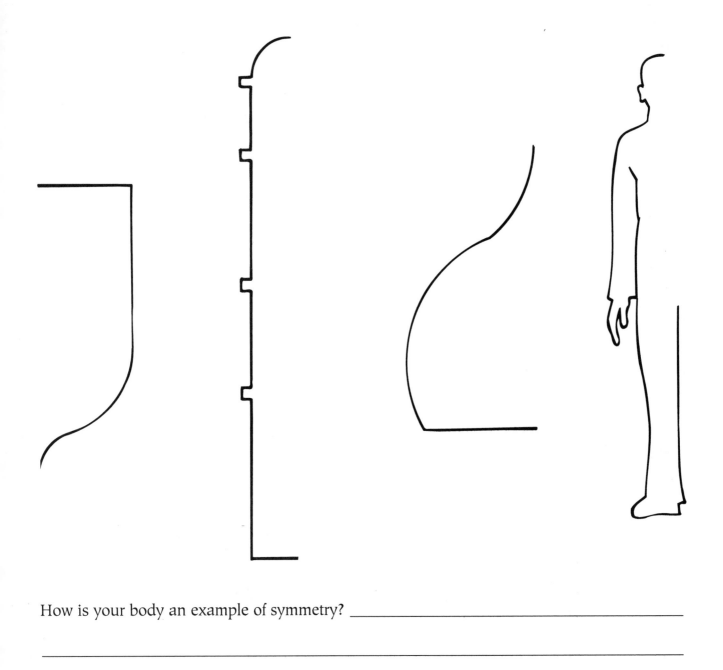

How is your body an example of symmetry? _____

_____

_____

The Waiotapu Thermal Wonderland

The Waiotapu Thermal Wonderland is located about thirty minutes outside the city of Rotorua on the north island of New Zealand. This small city is a center for tourism because of **geothermal** activity in the area. It is built on an active volcanic **fault line** and surrounded by lakes, volcanoes, and great natural beauty.

Waiotapu means "sacred waters" in the Maori language. Visitors can walk among **geysers**, mud pools, and smoking **fumaroles**. The Champagne Pools are colored yellow and orange. The colors are caused by mineral salts in the water. Beyond the pools there is a spectacular multicolored waterfall. The colors are caused by chemicals and minerals in the water.

Every morning, about 10:00 a.m., the Lady Knox Geyser fires a **plume** of smoke. It is rumored that a guide causes this eruption by putting a little soap powder down the **blowhole**. There are craters at Waiotapu with boiling **sulphur** springs. The Inferno Crater has a bottom of boiling mud, and the Artist's Palette has many colors in its hot and cold pools.

Another important geothermal site, Whakarewarewa, is located near Waiotapu. It has 500 hot springs and pools of **silica** and mineral deposits. This area has the largest geyser in New Zealand, called Pohutu. It erupts about 15 times a day.

Answer in complete sentences:

1. Why would a tourist want to visit Rotorua?

2. Name three examples of geothermal activity at Waiotapu.

3. Why is the Lady Knox Geyser special?

4. Why are the waters of Waiotapu brightly colored?

5. What is Pohutu? How often does it erupt?

Web site:
nz.com/tour/Rotorua/Waiotapu.html

Science

You will need:

✔ encyclopedia (volume G)
✔ paper
✔ pencil

Draw a diagram of a geyser and explain how geysers are formed. Why do they erupt?

Geography

You will need:

✔ world map
✔ atlas
✔ paper
✔ pencil

Locate the north and south islands of New Zealand on a map of the world. What are the latitude and longitude lines for Wellington, Auckland, Christchurch, and Dunedin?

Social Studies

You will need:

✔ nonfiction information about New Zealand
✔ paper
✔ pencil

How are the Maori people important to the history of New Zealand? Write a description of the people and three important facts about their culture.

Science

You will need:

✔ nonfiction information about minerals
✔ chart paper
✔ pencil

Make a chart showing the names of common minerals and their colors.

The Waiotapu Thermal Wonderland

Word Search Puzzle

```
T W R I F R N E W Z E A L A N D T R
O A N S P M I O E S M L O D E R E F
E I S I L L T E O E L A S E T T A I
T O B I R M U Y D A N O O O A R H G
R T L Y T O E M F E A L N R A U V T
M A O S G N T R E S D O C S I A O N
J P W A E H E A L N I A O L D U L E
W U H N E T O O A T E A A E P E C E
N S O H A G O L P R E M N E R A A F
H T L W O P R U R L R I G R M R N C
I E E N S E R E O E L O U E B A O M
D E A D D E U R H T S H T E Y I E I
E T H N H S A T L E P M P O E S S N
H S O R H M O U O L R G O R R M E E
E W H E U E A I U E O C H N U U O R
S M V F G F E S M A A B U G C T A A
E A D S N E M I P M T A T E I E A L
E R O B T E A T R M E E U R E E T S
```

Look for these words:

GEOTHERMAL

PLUME

GEYSER

CRATER

ERUPTION

FUMAROLE

WATERFALL

NEW ZEALAND

WAIOTAPU

ROTORUA

MAORI

MINERALS

POHUTU

ERUPT

WONDERLAND

VOLCANOES

POOLS

SULPHUR

BLOWHOLE

FAULT LINE

Europe

Europe is smaller than every other continent in the world except Australia. It is located on the western side of the world's largest landmass, which includes both Asia and Europe (sometimes called Eurasia). The boundaries of Europe extend from the Arctic Ocean in the north to the Mediterranean Sea in the south, and from the Atlantic Ocean in the west to the Ural Mountains in the east. Europe is divided into 47 countries, including the largest country in the world, Russia, and the smallest, Vatican City. About 713 million people live in Europe.

Beginning with the early Greek and Roman civilizations, Europeans have made important contributions to government, art, and science. The Industrial Revolution (1700) began in Europe and marked the start of manufacturing around the world. Many European countries kept colonies in Africa and Asia in order to have enough raw materials and a market for their manufactured goods.

Europe has areas of natural beauty and fertile farmland. There are mountain ranges and grassy plains. Rivers provide electricity, irrigation, and transportation routes. About one-sixth of the people earn their living through farming. Farmers, helped by mild climates, good rainfall, and modern equipment, produce more crops per acre than anywhere in the world.

Some of the largest and more famous cities of the world are in Europe. London, Paris, and Rome are major cities with cathedrals, palaces, museums, landmarks, and ancient ruins that attract visitors from all parts of the world. The Swiss Alps, French Riviera, Black Forest, and tulip fields of the Netherlands are all part of Europe's natural beauty.

World War I (1914–1918) and World War II (1939–1945) began in Europe. The wars destroyed property and cost many lives. They brought about changes in the governments of many countries. Eastern European countries were ruled by Communists until the end of 1991 when the Soviet Union collapsed.

In 1993, 15 Western European countries formed a group called the European Union. The headquarters for the European Union is in Brussels, Belgium.

The Alhambra

The Alhambra was a **fortress** built in 1240 by the Moors, a Muslim people from Africa. It is located in the city of Granada, Spain. Built of red brick, the original Alhambra was a group of houses, schools, baths, **barracks**, and gardens. Today, all that remains is the Royal Palace and the Alcazaba fortress.

The Royal Palace is built of wood, tile, and **stucco**. Beautifully painted **plaster** moldings cover the walls and ceilings. These materials were not meant to last so the palace has been added to and changed by rulers over the years. Outside, the Courtyard of the Lions is famous for its carved **pillars** and **ornate** fountain.

Alhambra was in ruins at the beginning of the 17th century. The city of Granada began restoring the grounds and buildings in 1862.

A visitor can enter the Alhambra **complex** at the ruins of Alcazaba. A nearby bell tower, the Torre de la Vela, offers a wonderful view of the surrounding area. The Palace of Charles V is a square building with a round inner **courtyard**. This palace was once used for bullfights; today it is the site of concerts.

The Royal Palace has three sections. One section has offices where government business was conducted. In the second section, the sultan held court and entertained visitors. The third section of the palace has the apartments of the sultan and his family.

Alhambra was captured by the forces of Ferdinand and Isabella for Spain in 1492. It is now a national monument.

Answer in complete sentences:

1. What building materials were used in the Royal Palace?

2. Why do you think the Royal Place was built to be changed over the years?

3. What does a visitor to the Alhambra see?

4. What activities take place in the courtyard of the Palace of Charles V?

5. Who lived in the Royal Palace at Alhambra?

Web site:
tuspain.com/alhambra.htm

Creative Writing

You will need:
- ✔ paper
- ✔ pencil

Pretend that you are the sultan in the year 1250. What three decrees (laws) could you make to improve the lives of your subjects?

What problems do you think the workers experienced renovating the Royal Palace? What probably needed to be fixed? How would the job be easier in modern times?

Art

You will need:
- ✔ art supplies
- ✔ pictures of the Alhambra

Build a model of the Alhambra complex. You may include the ruins of Alcazaba, the bell tower, bathhouse, gardens, and Royal Palace.

Language Arts

You will need:
- ✔ list of vocabulary words from page 87
- ✔ dictionary
- ✔ writing paper
- ✔ pencil

Choose five of the words from the list to include in an original story.

Look up the definitions for the vocabulary words in your dictionary. Make a list showing the part of speech for each one.

Social Studies

You will need:
- ✔ travel book about Spain
- ✔ map of Spain
- ✔ pencil

Locate Granada on a map of Spain.

What would a tourist see on a visit to Granada? Do you think it would be a good place to live? Explain.

Locate five other Spanish castles. Mark their names and locations on the map.

The Alhambra

Using information from the article, write and draw something that could have happened in each section of the Royal Palace at Alhambra.

The Channel Tunnel

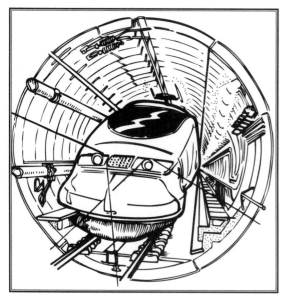

The "Eurotunnel," as it is called, is actually three tunnels that run under the English Channel. There are two rail tunnels and a service tunnel. The system was completed in 1994, the result of a joint effort linking Great Britain with the European **continent.** It connects Folkestone, England and Calais, France. Before the tunnel, travelers had to cross the English Channel by **ferry**. There are no bridges across the **channel.**

In 1985 the British and French governments began looking at plans to build the underwater transportation system. English workers began digging toward France in December 1987, and the French began digging from the opposite direction three months later. They continued at a rate of about one mile (1.6 km) per month using boring machines with teeth made of **tungsten** steel. These machines were able to cut through the chalk marl (a soft rock made of chalk and clay) that runs under the water. The tunnels are about 150 feet (46 m) below the water. Workers broke through the ends of the tunnels by June 28, 1991.

Seven months later, all three tunnels were connected and ready for railroad tracks. The Channel Tunnel was opened by Queen Elizabeth II and French President Mitterrand on May 6, 1994.

It is now possible to cross the English Channel using high-speed Eurostar passenger trains. Two lines connect London with Brussels and Paris. The more popular method, Le Shuttle (rail carriages), runs 24 hours a day and requires passengers to stay inside or near their cars. The $15 billion Eurotunnel, built with public funds, has been in financial trouble since its opening.

Answer in complete sentences:

1. What do you think is the purpose of the service tunnel?

2. How was the Eurotunnel built?

3. What happened on May 6, 1994?

4. What means of crossing the English Channel are available to travelers?

5. What kind of people do you think would or would not use the Eurotunnel?

Web site:
www.raileurope.com/erstw1.htm

Research

You will need:
- ✔ nonfiction books about Japan
- ✔ encyclopedia (volumes J and T)
- ✔ paper
- ✔ pencil

Compare and contrast the Channel Tunnel with the Seikan Tunnel in Japan. (It is a longer tunnel, but not so much of it is underwater.)

Math

You will need:
- ✔ a map of the United States
- ✔ pencil
- ✔ paper
- ✔ calculator

Determine the number of days necessary to bore a tunnel between two locations (of your choice) at the rate of one mile (1.6 km) per thirty days.

Creative Writing

You will need:
- ✔ nonfiction books about water transportation
- ✔ writing paper and pencil

Would you prefer to cross the English Channel by the Eurotunnel or ferry? Explain.

What is the tunnel's value to the British?

Social Studies

You will need:
- ✔ paper and pencil

What kinds of jobs were created because of the Eurotunnel and Eurostar trains? What general statements can be made about the effect of the Eurotunnel on the economy of Europe?

The Channel Tunnel

Word Search Puzzle

```
L E T D E S E R C A E E T W T E E T
H P T S I O A T D H C N S E T N L N
O E A A B T H A E A A G R L O G E F
E M L S S O N F N E C L A O A L D U
L A J O S A R P R B T I K R D A M N
C I R H E E E I O A U S D M E N S D
O U N E I E N E N R N H A A A D S E
E O T K F T R G E G A C E A A R E R
E S H I I A B W E T M H E T E S L W
R E T R A N S P O R T A T I O N I A
F I T E N I G H N H A N C U A H E T
E D S A I N S T S U O N D H N E J E
R O O L E S H U T T L E E N I N O R
R H I G H S P E E D R L I I D N E O
Y M H N R A I L R O A D D E E C E L
E N I E A O E F O L K E S T O N E S
K O E C E T Y O E M N O N T T I U P
D E T U N G S T E N S T E E L R E T
```

Can you find these words?

TUNNEL

FERRY

LINKING

ENGLISH CHANNEL

TUNGSTEN STEEL

CHALK MARL

EUROSTAR

RAILROAD

FOLKESTONE

CALAIS

UNDERWATER

TRANSPORTATION

BORING MACHINES

PASSENGER

ENGLAND

FRANCE

HIGH SPEED

LE SHUTTLE

The Colosseum

The Colosseum was an **arena** built for the entertainment of the Roman people. It was 187 feet (57 m) high and had four levels of seating. The open top could be covered by a huge **awning.** As early as the third century B.C., Roman builders discovered a way to make **concrete** by mixing **mortar** with gravel, sand, and rubble. This was a cheaper and more convenient building material than cut stone. Concrete was used with metal frames to strengthen the Colosseum as early as A.D. 70. It took ten years for a large group of slaves to complete the **massive** structure. The Colosseum still stands in the center of modern Rome.

The Colosseum held 50,000 **spectators** who entered the arena through 80 gates. They were seated by social class, with women and children far away from the action in the top rows. Everyone needed to buy a ticket to attend the games, much as we do today.

Criminals or slaves called **gladiators** were trained to fight to the death as entertainment for the crowds. The **emperor** was proud of the skills and courage of his fighters. A **maze** of passageways led to hundreds of animal pens below the floor of the arena. Gladiators fought each other or wild animals on foot or from horseback.

Sometimes the floor of the Colosseum was flooded and **naval** battles were fought. After the cruelest events were **banned,** other sporting events at the Colosseum included **archery** matches, bull fighting, boxing, and **chariot** races. The Colosseum was dedicated by Emperor Titus in A.D. 80 with 100 days of games.

Though the Colosseum is now in **ruins**, it is still one of the Romans' greatest achievements and most famous landmarks. It draws thousands of tourists each year.

Answer in complete sentences:

1. Describe what was involved in building the Colosseum.

2. How did the invention of concrete and use of metal framing change the construction business?

3. Explain the job of a gladiator.

4. What events did Colosseum spectators attend?

Web sites:
www.city.net/countries/italy/rome
pharos.bu.edu/Egypt/Wonders/Forgotten/colosseum.html

Creative Writing

You will need:
- ✔ paper
- ✔ pencil

Write a newspaper article telling factual information about the building of a stadium or a sporting event held near you.

Social Studies

You will need:
- ✔ tourist information about Rome
- ✔ atlas
- ✔ encyclopedia (volumes I and R)

Make a list of other famous Roman landmarks. Choose one that interests you and make a drawing or write a brief description of it.

Language Arts

You will need:
- ✔ list of the vocabulary words from page 93
- ✔ dictionary
- ✔ writing paper
- ✔ pencil

Choose five of the words from the list to include in an original story.

Look up the definitions for the vocabulary words in your dictionary. Make a list, showing the part of speech for each one.

Art

You will need:
- ✔ large white drawing paper
- ✔ markers or crayons

Work with a partner to design a poster for an event at the Colosseum. Be sure to indicate the location, date, time, and cost of the event. Display your poster in the center.

The Colosseum

I am located in the capital city of Italy.

I am very near the Colosseum.

I was built on a swamp on the east bank of the Tiber River.

I was the center of ancient Roman government and business.

I am the place where Anthony delivered the funeral oration for Caesar before Caesar was cremated.

My ruins are now a famous tourist attraction. There are marble pillars and arches which indicate the markets, temples, and government buildings of ancient Rome.

What am I? _____
          (answer: Forum)

The Eiffel Tower

The Eiffel Tower was built in 1889 by Alexandre-Gustave Eiffel for the World's Fair. It rises 984 feet (300 m) into the air on a frame of iron **girders**. There are three main **platforms** which can be reached from stairs or elevators. It is a high **observation** point and the best-known landmark in Paris, drawing 3.5 million visitors each year. Guided tours are popular with tourists.

The first level of the structure has a theater which shows a short movie about the tower's history. There are also a **café**, restaurant, gallery, post office, and souvenir shops to attract tourists. Many visitors take home reminders of the famous landmark.

A private elevator takes patrons to a fancy restaurant on the second level. Many enjoy a delicious dinner and the chance to see Paris by night. There is a garden under the Eiffel Tower. The Champs-de-Mars is a gathering place for Parisians during holiday festivals.

It is interesting to note that for a time, after the 1889 exposition, many Parisians wanted to tear down the Eiffel Tower because they thought it was ugly. Fortunately, the landmark was saved because it was valuable as a radio-telegraph center during World War I. The government declared the Eiffel Tower a national site in January 1964.

Answer in complete sentences:

1. When was the Eiffel Tower built? Why was it built and by whom?

2. What Parisian landmarks might you see from the observation decks of the Eiffel Tower?

3. How did the invention of elevators encourage the building of skyscrapers? Explain.

4. Have you ever visited a skyscraper? Explain your experience.

Web site:
www.paris.org/Monuments/Eiffel

Creative Writing

You will need:
- lined paper
- drawing paper
- markers
- pencils

Visit an observation point near you. It may be the top of a hill or the roof of a building. Make a drawing and write about what you see.

Math

You will need:
- nonfiction books about skyscrapers

Make a list of ten skyscrapers organized by height (shortest to tallest). Indicate the heights in feet and meters.

Science

You will need:
- nonfiction books about skyscrapers
- clay
- cardboard scraps
- pencil
- drinking straws
- ruler
- scissors

Study the books to determine what must be considered before building a skyscraper. Use the drinking straws, clay, and cardboard to create a model of the Eiffel Tower. (Connect the straws by inserting one inside of the other.)

Another day, try to build the highest tower possible from the same supplies.

Social Studies

You will need:
- encyclopedia (volume P)
- nonfiction books about Paris

Make a list of Paris landmarks that you think can be seen from the observation deck of the Eiffel Tower. Choose one to draw or write about. Display your work in the center.

The Eiffel Tower

Crossword Puzzle

ACROSS

2. Function of the Eiffel Tower during WWI
4. In 1964, the French government declared the Eiffel Tower a _____ site.
6. Best-known landmark in France
11. Builder of the Eiffel Tower
13. The Eiffel Tower is built on a frame of iron ___.
14. ___ tours are popular with tourists.

DOWN

1. Gathering place for Parisians during holiday festivals
3. The Eiffel Tower was built for the ___ ___.
5. The Eiffel Tower measures 300 ___ high.
7. Country where the Eiffel Tower is located
8. The first level of the Eiffel Tower has a ___.
9. City where the Eiffel Tower is located
10. Patrons can take a private ___ to a restaurant on the second level of the Eiffel Tower.
12. Number of platforms on the Eiffel Tower

Hagia Sophia

Hagia Sophia was built in Istanbul (**formerly** Constantinople), Turkey by the emperor Justinian in A.D. 537. For 900 years, it was the main Christian church of the Byzantine Empire. In the mid-1400s, the city was conquered by the Turks and the church became a **mosque**. Hagia Sophia has been a museum since 1935.

Hagia Sophia is best known for its round center **dome** set on a square, **minarets**, and richly decorated **interior**. The original **mosaics** and **frescoes** of religious figures were plastered over by the Turks. The art work has now been uncovered and restored.

The original **bronze** gates still stand at the entrance of Hagia Sophia. Inside the church is a Moslem **pulpit**, and the **apse** which faces Mecca. There is a great central dome and half domes supported by eight green marble **pillars** on the sides of the center aisle. The interior domes are decorated with paintings of religious figures.

Many people believe the outside of the massive structure is best viewed from a ferry boat on the Marmara Sea.

Answer in complete sentences:

1. In what year did Hagia Sophia become a museum?

2. Why does the apse face Mecca?

3. How is the interior of Hagia Sophia decorated?

4. Why would it be best to view a building like the Hagia Sophia from a distance?

Web site:
www.duke.edu/~emin/ISTANBUL/PLACES/ayasofya.html

Art

You will need:
- ✔ encyclopedia (volume B)
- ✔ scraps of colored construction paper
- ✔ glue stick
- ✔ white drawing paper
- ✔ pencil

Design and create a mosaic in the style of Byzantine artists.

Social Studies

You will need:
- ✔ nonfiction information about Turkey
- ✔ paper
- ✔ pencil

How does the Muslim religion affect the traditions and culture of Turkey?

How does the appearance of Hagia Sophia differ from other mosques around the world? (Grand Mosque at Djenne, Al-Haram, etc.)

Creative Writing

You will need:
- ✔ nonfiction information about Turkey
- ✔ paper
- ✔ pencil

What would your life be like if you were a Turkish child? How would life be different for a boy or a girl?

Research

You will need:
- ✔ nonfiction information about Turkey
- ✔ paper
- ✔ pencil

The Blue Mosque is very near Hagia Sophia. Compare and contrast these two Turkish landmarks.

Hagia Sophia

Match the terms and definitions.

____ mosque

1. a tower on a mosque used for calling the people to prayer

____ dome

2. colored marble or glass chips set in cement to make pictures

____ minaret

3. a circular roof or ceiling

____ interior

4. a strong, freestanding column

____ mosaic

5. an Islamic place of worship

____ fresco

6. a domed projection of a church

____ bronze

7. painting done on fresh plaster

____ pulpit

8. the inside of a thing

____ pillar

9. an alloy of copper and tin

____ apse

10. a platform used in conducting a worship service

Answers: 5, 3, 1, 8, 2, 7, 9, 10, 4, 6

The Kremlin

The word *kreml* means fortress in Russian. The Moscow Kremlin is the center of Russian government. The buildings are surrounded by a wall. Ivan the Great hired Russian and Italian architects to create the city. Because Ivan was more interested in beauty than defense, the "Old Russian" style of architecture included irregular shapes and the well-known onion domes.

The appearance of the Kremlin has changed over the years. During the War of 1812, Napoleon's troops occupied the grounds for 35 days and tried to destroy the buildings. Townspeople were able to put out the fires. The Kremlin Palace and Armory were built in the mid-1800s. Vladimir Lenin wrote a law to protect the art works and monuments. He ordered the buildings restored and made into museums.

Visitors enter the Kremlin through a gate on the west side near the Armory Tower. It is the oldest museum in Russia. There are nine **exhibition** halls that trace the history of the country. On the first floor are displays of armor, weapons, and gold and silver pieces, including jewelry, watches, bowls, and **chalices**. There is also an important display of famous Fabergé eggs; one of them contains a **miniature** golden train that runs when it is wound with a key. Other valuable collections include the jeweled robes of Catherine the Great and Peter the Great.

On the ground floor are gold and silver gifts from foreign countries and a Throne and Crown Room with one throne that is covered with 2,000 jewels. The final displays are of saddles, bridles, and carriages used by royalty. The famous Orlov Diamond (189 carats), which was a gift to Catherine the Great, is exhibited in the Armory along with her **coronation** crown which is covered with almost 5,000 small diamonds.

Other points of interest on the Kremlin grounds include the Emperor Canon and the Emperor Bell. The Canon weighs 40 tons and the Bell weighs 210 tons. Pictures of Russia's **czars** are cast in the metal.

Answer in complete sentences:

1. Which ruler was in power when the Kremlin was built?

2. What would you be most interested in seeing at the Armory Tower?

3. Explain how the Kremlin was almost destroyed.

4. How did Vladimir Lenin help save the Kremlin?

Web site:
www.hyperion.com/~koreth/russia/Kremlin/

Art

You will need:
- ✔ pictures of several different Fabergé eggs
- ✔ paper
- ✔ pencil
- ✔ markers
- ✔ scissors
- ✔ glue
- ✔ black paper

Decide on a theme and design an original egg in the style of Fabergé. Cut it out and glue it to a black background paper for display. Write a description of your egg.

Social Studies

You will need:
- ✔ nonfiction information about Moscow
- ✔ pencil
- ✔ paper

Make a list of the points of interest in Red Square other than the buildings of the Kremlin. Choose one and explain its importance to Russian history.

Research

You will need:
- ✔ nonfiction books about London and Moscow
- ✔ paper
- ✔ pencil

Make a list of the similarities and differences between the Tower of London and the Armory Tower.

Social Studies

You will need:
- ✔ several different nonfiction sources of information about St. Basil's Cathedral
- ✔ paper
- ✔ pencil

Create a time line of events in the history of St. Basil's Cathedral using the information you have gathered. How is the building used today? How will it probably be used in the future?

Kremlin

Crossword

ACROSS

3. The Emperor ___ weighs 210 tons.
5. City where the Kremlin is located
6. The Emperor ___ weighs 40 tons.
10. The Armory Tower has a collection of jeweled robes of ___ ___ ___.
11. Famous 189-carat diamond
12. Country where the Kremlin is located
15. Kind of eggs found in the Armory Tower
16. Kind of dome in russian architecture
18. The Kremlin buildings are surrounded by a ___.
19. Catherine's ___ crown has nearly 5,000 diamonds.
20. Czar who created the Kremlin

DOWN

1. Built in the mid-1800s
2. English meaning of the *kreml*
4. He wrote a law to protect the Kremlin art works and monuments.
7. The center of the Russian government
8. Another name for goblets located on the first floor of the Armory Tower
9. Ivan the Great hired Russian and ___ architects to create the Kremlin.
13. Pictures of Russia's czars are cast in ___.
14. Oldest museum in Russia
17. French commander whose troops occupied the Kremlin grounds

Neuschwanstein Castle

Neuschwanstein Castle was built by King Ludwig II of Bavaria when he was the ruler of Germany. He and his brother had grown up at Hohenschwangau Castle. When Ludwig's father (Maxmillian II) died, the young man was not prepared to rule the country. He chose to spend his time and fortune creating **fantasy** castles. Because of this, Ludwig II is sometimes called the Fairy-Tale King.

Neuschwanstein, which took 17 years to build, was designed to look like a **medieval** castle with towers, **turrets**, **parapets**, and **battlements**. All of these items were decorative, since there was no need to defend the castle. The building had a central heating system and hot and cold running water in the kitchen. Unfortunately, King Ludwig drowned in 1886 before his throne room was completed.

Ludwig was a friend and supporter of the composer Richard Wagner. He used the stories from his operas as the theme for many rooms of the castle. The walls of the Great Parlor have paintings showing the story of the opera *Lohengrin*. The Singers' Hall is decorated with characters from *Tannhauser* and *Parsifal,* and the King's private rooms are decorated in the style of *Tristan and Isolde.* These operas were favorites of King Ludwig.

Ludwig lived at Neuschwanstein Castle for less than six months. Nevertheless, the story of his life and the castles built during his rule continue to be very popular with German tourists.

Answer in complete sentences:

1. Who was Richard Wagner? Why was he important to King Ludwig II?

2. What modern conveniences were built into Neuschwanstein Castle?

3. What operas are depicted in paintings on the castle walls?

4. How do Ludwig's castles benefit the German economy?

5. How long did Ludwig live at Neuschwanstein Castle?

Web site:
www.could-nine.co.uk/emeric/neusch.htm

Research

You will need:

- ✔ nonfiction books about Europe and castles
- ✔ chart paper
- ✔ markers

Make a list of 25 castles of Europe. Classify your list by country.

Art

You will need:

- ✔ pictures of castles
- ✔ art supplies
- ✔ white paper

Make a drawing of a medieval castle with towers, turrets, parapets, and battlements.

Language Arts

You will need:

- ✔ nonfiction information about opera stories
- ✔ paper
- ✔ pencil
- ✔ crayons
- ✔ markers
- ✔ book cover

Choose an opera by Richard Wagner. Write a summary of the story. Make drawings of the main characters. Bind your pages in a book. Design an appropriate cover.

Social Studies

You will need:

- ✔ travel books about Germany
- ✔ map of Germany
- ✔ pencil

Locate and label these castles of Ludwig II: Linderhof, Herrenchiemsee, Hohenschwangau.

Neuschwanstein Castle

Think of five questions you would like to ask Ludwig II about his interest in building castles. Write them here:

1. _____

2. _____

3. _____

4. _____

5. _____

Pass your paper to a friend. Ask her or him to answer your questions as King Ludwig II might have done.

_____

Ludwig designed the rooms of Neuschwanstein around the stories of Richard Wagner's operas. Choose a song whose words you know. What kinds of paintings or art objects could you design for a room that would fit the meaning of your song? Draw your ideas here.

The Parthenon

The Parthenon is one of the largest and most beautiful of all the Greek temples. It was built in the fifth century B.C. and dedicated to the **goddess** Athena. The Parthenon, designed by Greek architects Ictinus and Callicrates, is located on a hill called the Acropolis in the center of Athens. About A.D. 500, it became a Christian church. In the mid-1400s Turkish Moslems captured Athens and the Parthenon served as a **mosque**.

The Turks stored gunpowder inside the Parthenon. The inside of the building was blown up when the Venetians tried to conquer the city in 1687.

The Greek style of architecture creates buildings with clean lines and balanced shapes. The builders developed new ways to hold heavy roofs in place with support beams around the outside and through the center. They were the first to use **wrought iron** in their buildings.

The Parthenon is built of white marble. The **enclosed** space in the center is divided into two rooms. In one of the rooms there was a huge golden statue of the goddess Athena. On the outer walls there were **friezes** showing battles scenes from the Trojan War and **mythology**.

The Parthenon has a rectangular base with 46 **columns** around the 4 sides. Each column has 10–12 separate sections held in place with wooden plugs through the centers. The columns are decorated at the top in the Doric style.

Brightly-painted sculptures once filled the Parthenon. Most of these were destroyed in the 1687 explosion. Remaining sculpture from the Parthenon is displayed at museums in Athens and in London.

Answer in complete sentences:

1. What architects designed the Parthenon?

2. How was the Parthenon used in A.D. 500? the mid-1400s?

3. How are the columns constructed? decorated?

4. Where are the remaining sculptures from the Parthenon displayed?

Web site:
www.dilos.com/region/attica/acropolis_rock.html

Math

You will need:
- ✔ paper
- ✔ pencil

What is the area of the inside of the Parthenon with dimensions of 240' x 102' (73.2 x 31 m)? If the two inside rooms were of equal size, what would be the dimensions of each one?

Social Studies

You will need:
- ✔ nonfiction information about Greek mythology
- ✔ paper
- ✔ pencil
- ✔ markers
- ✔ book binding materials

Work with your friends to write one-page stories about the most important Greek gods. Illustrate your stories and bind them in a cover.

Art

You will need:
- ✔ encyclopedia (volume C)
- ✔ paper
- ✔ pencil

Copy pictures of the Greek Doric, Ionic, and Corinthian columns. How would you describe the Doric style?

Social Studies

You will need:
- ✔ nonfiction information about Greek history
- ✔ paper
- ✔ pencil
- ✔ drawing paper
- ✔ crayons
- ✔ markers

Write a story about the Trojan War giving details about the characters, problems, and solution. Make a drawing of the Trojan horse.

The Parthenon

Use an encyclopedia to complete this chart about Greek gods and goddesses.

Name	God or Goddess	Title
Zeus		
Apollo		
Poseidon		
Athena		
Hades		
Artemis		
Aphrodite		

Describe your idea of a religious service at the Parthenon in ancient Greece. Who would have attended? What might have taken place?

_____

_____

_____

_____

_____

_____

_____

The Sognefjorden

Fjords (fiords) are long, narrow bodies of water that are carved out of mountains by the movement of **glaciers**. Glaciers are mountains or large masses of ice that move very slowly. As the ice melts, sea water moves in and fills the space. There is often an area of **fertile** farmland near the edge of the water. There are many of these fjords in Norway.

The Sognefjorden, at 120 miles (193 km) long and 4,260 feet (1,298 m) deep, is the longest and deepest fjord in the world. Narrow fingers of water push out from the main fjord deep into the mountains. Waterfalls create **hydro-electric** power which is used as far away as Oslo and Germany.

The **county** of Sogn has been popular with tourists for many years because of its **unspoiled** beauty. There are small villages on both sides of the water where most of the people still make their living by farming or fishing. Today, visitors can enjoy a fjord **cruise. Ferries** and boats provide transportation between villages.

Answer in complete sentences:

1. What are glaciers?

2. How long and deep is the Sognefjorden?

3. How do the people in the villages make their living?

4. What is supplied by the waterfalls of the fjord?

Web site:
www.jyu.fi/~jonmak/kartta1.html

Geography

You will need:

✔ nonfiction information about Norway
✔ paper
✔ pencil

Trace a map of Norway. Color the fjords blue.

Label Oslo, Bergen, and Sogn counties.

Research

You will need:

✔ encyclopedia (volume G)
✔ paper and pencil

What are the two main kinds of glaciers? How do they differ?

Make two diagrams to show how glaciers shape the land.

Creative Writing

You will need:

✔ paper
✔ pencil

Write a story explaining events in a day of a ferry boat captain cruising the Sognefjorden.

Research

You will need:

✔ encyclopedia (volume F)
✔ paper
✔ pencil

Where are fjords located other than Norway?

The Sognefjorden

Formation of a Fjord
Describe what is happening in each picture.

_____

_____

_____

_____

_____

_____

_____

_____

_____

_____

_____

_____

Stonehenge

Stonehenge is located about 80 miles (129 km) west of London near the top of a hill on Salisbury Plain. It is one of many similar rings of stone in Great Britain, however, Stonehenge is special because there is no written record of its builders or its purpose. It is believed to have been built about 4,000 years ago.

Because the three parts of the monument differ from one another, it is thought that it was built by three different groups of people. There is an outer ring of large stones, surrounded by two rings of earth and a ditch. Some of the stones in the outer ring were once joined into an unbroken circle with **capstones,** or **lintels.**

A ring of smaller blue stones **(spotted dolerite)** lies inside the outer ring. Three giant capped stones still stand inside the ring of blue stones. A walkway leads to the circle. Forty stones in all remain in place. The largest of them weighs 40 tons and stands more than 24 feet (7.3 m) high.

It is a mystery where these stones came from because they are not like any natural stones in the area. No one knows how the stones were cut by people who had only **primitive** tools. We cannot be sure how the heavy stones were raised and set into the ground.

Some **theorists** believe that Stonehenge was **created** as a religious monument. Some believe it was a calendar because one of the tallest rocks marks the sunrise on the day of summer **solstice.** Still others believe it was a burial ground or war **memorial.**

It seems most likely that Stonehenge was used (if not built) by the Druids, an ancient religious **sect** that is still active in Great Britain today.

Answer in complete sentences:

1. Why do you believe Stonehenge was built?

2. Who were the Druids and what is their connection to Stonehenge?

3. How many stones are still in Stonehenge? How large are they?

4. How do you think the walkway leading to Stonehenge was used by the builders?

Web sites:

www2.ucsc.edu/people/trillian/stonehenge/circle.html

www.activemind.com/Mysterious/Topics/Stonehenge/index.html

Creative Writing

You will need:
- ✔ nonfiction information about Stonehenge and Easter Island
- ✔ paper
- ✔ pencil

How is Stonehenge similar to the statues on Easter Island?

Social Studies

You will need:
- ✔ nonfiction information about primitive humans
- ✔ paper
- ✔ pencil

Draw pictures of five primitive tools that might have been used by the people who built Stonehenge.

Language Arts

You will need:
- ✔ pencil
- ✔ markers
- ✔ drawing paper

Fold the drawing paper in half. Label one side "before" and the other side "after." Write a story and make drawings to show the changes that time, weather, and tourists have caused at Stonehenge.

Research

You will need:
- ✔ encyclopedia (volume D)
- ✔ paper
- ✔ pencil

Write five facts about the Druids.

Stonehenge
Crossword Puzzle

ACROSS

1. The outer ring is surrounded by earth and a ___.
3. Stonehenge is believed to have been built ___ thousand years ago.
6. Ring of blue stones
8. Number of stones in place at Stonehenge
9. Stonehenge might have been built as a ___.
11. A ___ leads to the circle of stones.
12. There is no written ___ of Stonehenge's purpose or builders.
15. Ring of stones on Salisbury Plain
16. Number of giant stones standing inside the ring of blue stones
17. The people who built Stonehenge had only ___ tools.

DOWN

1. Religious sect that used Stonehenge
2. Stonehenge is located ___ (direction) of London.
4. The largest stone at Stonehenge weighs 40 ___.
5. Stonehenge might have been built as a ___.
7. Country where Stonehenge is located
10. The outer ring stones were once joined by ___.
13. The stones at Stonehenge are placed in the shape of a ___.
14. One stone marks sunrise on the day of the summer ___.

The Tower of London and Tower Bridge

The Tower of London is located beside the Thames River on the east side of London. The towers and **fortifications** were built by William the Conqueror to protect the city. The **fortress** is surrounded by a **moat**. Over the years it has served as a prison, palace, zoo, and the Royal **Mint**. The Tower is considered the most historic **monument** in England.

The grounds are guarded by the Yeoman Warders. Throughout its history, the Tower of London has been the site of **imprisonment** and **execution** for many of England's most famous prisoners. It currently houses the British Crown Jewels and the Tower Armories.

In the Jewel House, the visitor can see the exquisite Imperial State Crown, made for the **coronation** of Queen Victoria in 1838. It contains two very large stones, a ruby and a diamond, as well as over 3,000 smaller precious stones, mainly diamonds and pearls. In addition there are several **orbs** and **scepters** on display which are used in royal ceremonies.

The Tower Armories, established before 1600, are the oldest museums in England. Examples of **mail** and plate body armor in many different styles as well as helmets, shields, and weapons used since the Middle Ages recall the early period of England's history. Some of the armor was made for horses to wear in battle. In the Sporting Gallery is the King's **arsenal** of swords, **crossbows,** and fire arms.

The Tower Bridge is also a landmark symbol of London. This **drawbridge,** built between 1886 and 1894, is on the eastern end of the Thames River. It is designed so that large ships can pass under its raised roadway. There are towers at the north and south ends. The original powerhouse, in the southern tower, has been made into a small museum.

Answer in complete sentences:

1. What functions has the Tower of London served over the years?

2. What can a visitor see in the Jewel House?

3. What can a visitor see in the Royal Armories?

4. What is unusual about the design of the Tower Bridge?

Web sites:

www.city.net/countries/england/london
www.voicenet.com/%7Edravyk/toltour/

Research

You will need:

✔ nonfiction books about the Tower of London and history of England

Write a paragraph about the problems of some of the Tower's famous prisoners: Anne Boleyn, Sir Walter Raleigh, Thomas Cromwell, Sir Thomas More, Lady Jane Grey, Guy Fawkes.

Science

You will need:

✔ nonfiction books about bridges and architecture

Make drawings and write information about the operation of a drawbridge.

Art

You will need:

✔ art supplies
✔ nonfiction materials about the Tower of London

Design a crown, helmet, shield, or sword like the ones displayed at the Tower of London.

Social Studies

You will need:

✔ nonfiction books about Europe
✔ paper
✔ pencil

Locate and list five other European fortresses. Choose one to explain in a paragraph.

The Tower of London and Tower Bridge

The Ravens

There is a 300-year-old legend that says the British nation will disappear when the last raven has left the grounds of the Tower of London. Therefore, six of the birds (with clipped wings) are carefully guarded by the Yeoman Raven Master. They roam the Tower Green, have private houses, and are fed a controlled diet. One of the oldest of the Tower birds, named Jim Crow, lived 44 years.

Read more about ravens and answer these questions.

1. How are they the same or different than crows? Describe their physical appearance.

    _____

    _____

    _____

2. Where do they live? _____

    What do they eat? _____

3. Explain the nesting behavior of ravens. _____

    _____

    _____

4. What other symbols or legends are associated with ravens? _____

    _____

(Read *The Raven* by Edgar Allan Poe.)

Vatican City

Vatican City has been the world's smallest independent country since 1929. Located inside Rome, Italy, this walled city-state is the home of the Pope and the headquarters of the Roman Catholic Church. In an area less than .25 miles (.4 km), the Vatican has its own post office, bank, newspaper, radio station, and market. It prints its own stamps, coins, and license plates.

St. Peter's Square is the center of the Vatican City-State. Visitors usually fill the large, open space decorated with **columns** and **monuments**. There is an Egyptian **obelisk** from the first century B.C. in the center of the square. Tourists shop for souvenirs just beyond the square at the edge of the city. Each Sunday morning, the Pope speaks to the crowds from the window of the **papal** apartment.

St. Peter's Basilica is one of the largest and most **magnificent** of all the Roman Catholic churches. Built on the burial place of St. Peter, the **basilica** contains important sculpture, artwork, and religious **relics** of great value.

The Vatican Palace contains over 1,000 rooms. There are **chapels**, apartments, **reception** rooms, offices, and museums as well as private courtyards. Inside the Palace are the Vatican Museums which contain the world's largest collection of antique art and statues. The most famous room in the palace is the Sistine Chapel. Paintings by Michelangelo decorate the ceiling of the chapel.

Answer in complete sentences:

1. Describe St. Peter's Square.

2. What will a visitor find in the Vatican Palace?

3. How was the location for St. Peter's Basilica chosen?

4. When does the Pope speak to the people gathered in St. Peter's Square?

Web site:
www.city.net/vatican_city/

Social Studies

You will need:
- ✓ nonfiction information and tourist brochures about Avignon, France
- ✓ paper
- ✓ pencil

Learn more about Avignon, France. It was once the home of the Pope. What remains of the papal palace in Avignon today? Of what importance is Avignon to the history of the Church?

Art

You will need:
- ✓ encyclopedia (volume F)
- ✓ paper
- ✓ pencil
- ✓ yellow crayon or marker

Make a drawing of the flag of Vatican City.

Research

You will need:
- ✓ biographies and research books about Italian artists
- ✓ paper
- ✓ pencil

Read about these Italian artists: Michelangelo, Raphael, Leonardo da Vinci, Titian, and Bernini.

Chart the years of their lives and the cities of their birth.

List two famous works for each one.

Geography

You will need:
- ✓ atlas
- ✓ paper
- ✓ pencil

Name the next three smallest countries in the world and list their sizes and populations.

Vatican City

Use an encyclopedia to complete this chart about places of worship around the world.

Building	Religion	Name	Location
Basilica	Roman Catholic	St. Peter's	Vatican City
Mosque			
Cathedral			
Basilica			
Church			
Temple			
Shrine			
Synagogue			
Pagoda			

Answer:
How have the contributions of Roman architects (domes, vaults, and arches) been used in places of worship around the world?

_____

_____

_____

Draw an example of each one:

Arch   **Vault**   **Dome**

Venice

Venice, Italy, is a city of 120 islands in the Adriatic Sea. It has canals instead of streets. There are no buses, trucks, or cars—only boats. The *industrial* centers of Marghera and Mestre on the Italian mainland are also part of the city. Venice is one of Italy's largest **ports**.

Centuries ago, Venice had control of trade in the eastern Mediterranean Sea. It was one of the largest cities in Europe and was part of an **empire** that included Crete, Cyprus, and the Dalmatian coast. In the late 1400s, Christopher Columbus "discovered" America and trade routes moved to the Atlantic Ocean. The power of Venice **declined** and it became part of Italy in 1866.

A **lagoon** separates the islands of Venice from the Italian mainland. Visitors must take ferry boats across the Grand Canal to the city. **Gondolas** are available to take tourists on a memorable canal ride. More than 400 bridges link the islands for foot traffic. All food, mail, and supplies are delivered by boat. Some people live on houseboats anchored on the canals.

Saint Mark's Square is the city center. The Basilica of St. Mark and the Doge's Palace stand on an open square facing St. Mark's Canal. The walks are lined with **cafes** and shops for tourists.

The Lido, a **sandbar** that borders the islands on the east, is one of Europe's most famous beach resorts. The Lido is also Venice's center for sports, including water sports, riding, tennis, and golf. There are few parks or gardens in Venice because space is limited.

Area craftspeople take advantage of the large tourist market in Venice. The island of Murano is famous for **crystal** and glassware. Burano, another island, is well known for lace and **embroidered** fabrics.

Answer in complete sentences:

1. How do people travel in Venice?

2. What two islands produce crafts for sale to tourists?

3. What is the Lido?

4. What islands were part of the Venetian Empire?

5. What would you see if you were sitting on St. Mark's Square?

Web site:
www.city.net/countries/italy/venice

Creative Writing

You will need:
- ✔ travel information about Venice
- ✔ paper
- ✔ pencil

What do you think life would be like living on a houseboat anchored in a Venetian canal?

Science

You will need:
- ✔ nonfiction information about pollution
- ✔ paper
- ✔ pencil

Summarize the effects of air and water pollution on the buildings and monuments of Venice.

If you were on a citizens' committee to improve environmental conditions in Venice, what would you suggest?

Geography

You will need:
- ✔ atlas or globe

Locate Italy and Venice. Draw a map of Italy and mark Rome, Venice, and three other major cities.

Locate Marghera and Mestre on the Italian mainland.

Locate Crete, Cyprus, and the Dalmatian coast.

Art

You will need:
- ✔ large white paper
- ✔ pencil
- ✔ markers

Design a tourist poster for the islands of Burano and Murano. Be sure to show examples of the craft items available in those locations.

Venice

Industries in Marghera and Mestre are a major reason for the air and water pollution that threatens Venice. In 1966, a major flood caused millions of dollars of damage to paintings and statues in Venice. Pollution threatens to slowly destroy the city and its treasures.

Choose one topic, circle it, and explain how it could affect the environment of Venice. What economic and social changes might occur?

erosion   **flood waters**   **air pollution**   **water pollution**

_____

_____

_____

_____

_____

_____

What could be done to stop or slow the deterioration?

_____

_____

_____

_____

_____

_____

_____

The Vienna State Opera House

The Vienna State Opera House, built by Eduard van der Nüll and August von Sicardsburg between 1861 and 1869, was the first building completed on Vienna's Ringstrasse. It is the home of the famous Vienna Philharmonic Orchestra. Each year their New Year's concert is broadcast around the world. The first opera performed at the Vienna State Opera House was Mozart's *Don Giovanni.*

The Opera House was destroyed during World War II and later **rebuilt** to its original appearance. Beethoven's opera *Fidelio* was chosen for the **reopening** performance on November 5, 1955.

The main hall has five **balconies** with seats for 1,642 people. There are 567 more places available for standing room. The stage is very deep, allowing plenty of room to build and store **scenery.** Employees dressed in **baroque** costumes greet tourists on the sidewalk in front of the hall with information about ticket sales. The **performances** are often sold out.

The most important social event of the year in Vienna is the Opera Ball, held each February. Women wearing elegant gowns and men in formal **attire** enjoy an evening of dancing in the ballroom.

Answer in complete sentences:

1. What are *Don Giovanni* and *Fidelio?*

2. How many people can attend a sold out performance at the Vienna State Opera House?

3. Why is the stage of the Vienna State Opera House so deep?

4. Whom is invited to attend the Opera Ball?

Web site:
www.city.net/countries/austria/vienna

Music

You will need:
- nonfiction information about classical music and composers
- art supplies
- paper
- pencil

Make a list of four composers who lived or performed in Vienna. Write a sentence to explain each person's contribution to the culture of the city.

Research

You will need:
- tourist information about Milan, Italy
- paper
- pencil

Write five facts about another famous European opera house, La Scala, in Milan, Italy.

Creative Writing

You will need:
- paper
- pencil

Pretend you are attending a performance at the Vienna State Opera House. What would you expect to see and hear?

Social Studies

You will need:
- tourist information about Vienna
- paper
- pencil

Name three buildings that a tourist will see on the Ringstrasse.

Write about one attraction you would like to visit in Vienna.

What famous hotel is located just across the street from the Opera House?

The Vienna State Opera House

Vienna was the center of European music in the 18th century. The city has memorials to these classical composers: Haydn, Mozart, Beethoven, Schubert, Brahms, and Johann and Richard Strauss.

Choose one of these composers and answer these questions.

Name of composer _____

What years did he live in Vienna?_____

List three compositions for which he is famous.

_____

_____

_____

If possible, describe his memorial(s) in Vienna.

_____

_____

Suppose you were an artist asked to design a memorial to this composer that would stand in the foyer of the Vienna State Opera House. What would you create and why?

(drawing)

_____

_____

_____

_____

_____

_____

North and South America

North America is the third largest continent in the world. It includes Canada, Greenland, the United States, Mexico, Central America, and the islands of the Caribbean Sea. The main language spoken in Canada, the United States, and many Caribbean Islands is English. The main language in Mexico and Central America is Spanish.

About 458 million people live in North America. The earliest people, Inuits, crossed the Bering Strait to North America following animals to hunt. In the 1500s, British, French, and Spanish explorers established colonies in the United States and Canada. African slaves were first brought to the Caribbean by the Spanish to work on sugar plantations. Most North Americans have ancestors who have immigrated from Europe, Asia, or Africa.

The temperatures of North America range from bitter cold in the Arctic to steamy hot in the tropics. Greenland is permanently covered by ice. In the treeless North American tundra, the temperature is seldom above freezing. Most of North America has mild to cold winters and warm to hot summers with moderate amounts of rain and snow.

South America is the fourth largest continent in the world. The equator crosses South America through Brazil, Columbia, and Ecuador. It is almost totally surrounded by water. A narrow strip of land called the Isthmus of Panama connects Central America with Columbia.

South America has almost every kind of climate and landscape. The world's largest rain forest, the Amazon Basin, covers two-fifths of the continent. There are also deserts, grasslands, mountains, and active volcanoes. It is an area of great natural beauty, with spectacular waterfalls, snow-covered mountains peaks, and varied plant and animal life.

There are 12 independent countries in South America. Because of the mountains, rain forests, and deserts, most of the major cities are located near the coast. The main language spoken in South America is Spanish.

The Amazon Rain Forest

The Amazon region in the north of Brazil covers two-fifths of the country. This area has the world's largest **tropical** rain forest. The average temperature is 80°F (27°C). The rain forest is very **humid**, receiving 87 inches (221 cm) of rainfall each year. It is home to many unusual kinds of plants and animals.

There are wild rubber trees, **mahogany, kapok,** and fig trees. Some of them grow very tall. Vines, **orchids, ferns,** and **cacti** grow on the bark of the trees, and fruits like **plantain, guava,** and **papaya** provide food for the animals and people living in the region.

The upper layer of the rain forest is called the **canopy.** It is home to more kinds of insects, animals, and birds than any other part of the rain forest. The canopy is so thick that many animals move about easily without ever touching the ground.

Many interesting animals, including **peccaries, sloth, armadillos, vampire bats, capybaras,** and **tapirs,** live in the rain forest. Many species of reptiles, such as the **anaconda** and the bush master, make the rain forest their home.

The Amazon River is the second longest river in the world. It flows out of the Andes Mountains across Brazil to the Atlantic Ocean. More than 2,500 kinds of fish live in the Amazon, including dangerous species like **piranhas, electric eels,** and **stingrays.**

Most people travel in the rain forest by boat or helicopter. There are few roads. Some native people are destroying the forest to graze their cattle. They want to farm the land. Wealthy land owners want to develop some of the land for industry. Scientists worry that this **deforestation** will threaten the region for years to come.

Answer in complete sentences:

1. What is the average rainfall and temperature in the Amazon rain forest?

2. Make a chart to show the names of mammals, fish, and reptiles that live in the rain forest.

3. What is the *canopy*?

4. How is the rain forest threatened?

Web site:
www.ran.org/ran/kids_action/index.html

Language Arts

You will need:
- ✔ Here is a list of rain forest animals and birds:

sloth	monkey	snake
porcupine	tapir	macaw
jaguar	anteater	toucan

Write a word to describe each animal or bird.

Research the names of ten other rain forest animals.

Art

You will need:
- ✔ art supplies
- ✔ shoe box

Stand the shoe box on end and design a diorama that shows the layers of a rain forest.

Creative Writing

You will need:
- ✔ paper
- ✔ pencil

Write a letter to:

Rain Forest Action Network
Suite 700
450 Sansome Street
San Francisco, California 94111

Ask about how your class can purchase and protect an acre of the rain forest.

Research

You will need:
- ✔ telephone number of your local weather service

What is your area's average temperature and rainfall in each season?

The Amazon Rain Forest

Addressing the Issue

Deforestation (burning or chopping down trees) is a major concern in the Amazon rain forest. Loggers are cutting down mahogany trees and building roads. Native people sometimes burn down the forests to make farmland. Loggers are able to make a great deal of illegal money selling rain forest products.

How do you feel about this problem? Do you think the United States should have a part in saving the rain forest? Complete the chart to organize you ideas. Write a short letter.

Issue: Deforestation

pros	cons
1. _____	1. _____
2. _____	2. _____
3. _____	3. _____

Write a letter to a United States official explaining your position on this issue.

Dear Sir or Madam:

My class is learning about the Amazon rain forest. I believe that destroying the trees in the rain forest *is or is not* a problem because _____

_____

_____

_____

_____

_____

_____

Sincerely,

Bonus - Oil has recently been discovered in the rain forest. Complete a similar chart and letter for the issue of oil spills and destruction because of building pipelines and refineries.

Brasília

Brasília is the capital city of Brazil. It was built near the center of the country to help **overcrowding** in the original capital of Rio de Janeiro. The idea for the city was first suggested in 1822 when Brazil became independent from Portugal, but construction did not begin until 1956. It took three years to build. Brasília was named the official capital in 1960.

Lúcio Costa designed a master plan for the city that included buildings, gardens, malls, and an artificial lake. Avenues were planned with **overpasses** and **underpasses** so that there would be no need for traffic lights. Another **architect**, Oscar Niemeyer, designed the public buildings.

Nearly all the building materials had to be flown to the site when construction began. Later, a highway was built, and in 1968, a railroad was completed. Today, an **international** airport also serves the city.

Brasília is shaped like an airplane with its nose facing Lake Paranoa. On the wings of the plane are blocks of high-rise apartment buildings made of concrete and glass. They form neighborhoods with schools, churches, shops, and parks. Between the wings, in the **fuselage** of the plane, there are government buildings and a downtown with banks, offices, hotels, cultural center, and the Cathedral of Brasília. Sports centers and light industries are located toward the tail section of the plane. A zoo, cemetery, and the airport are outside the city. Foreign embassies, a golf course, **yacht** club, and the University of Brasília are located around the nose of the plane near the lake. The Presidential Palace and other expensive private homes are built on land extending into the lake.

The city was originally meant for government business. Most of the people living there are government **employees**. It has also become a center for commerce and banking. Only light industry, such as food processing, arts and crafts, or printing, is allowed.

Answer in complete sentences:

1. Do you think the architects did a good job planning Brasília? Explain.

2. Why is only light industry permitted in Brasília?

3. What is most interesting to you about the design of the city? Explain.

4. What is located in the wings of the "plane"?

Web site:
www.geocities.com/TheTropics/3416

Language Arts

You will need:
- paper
- pencil

What kinds of knowledge and training did the architects of Brasília need before beginning their task? Why was pre-planning very important to their success?

Science

You will need:
- nonfiction books about Brazil
- paper
- pencil

Explain the weather and scenery in the interior of Brazil near the site of the capital.

Social Studies

You will need:
- paper
- pencil
- large white paper
- markers

Make a list of buildings and areas that you believe should be included in a perfectly planned city.

Research

You will need:
- encyclopedia (volumes B and R)
- other related nonfiction books
- paper
- pencil

Research information about the former capital of Brazil. How did moving the capital affect the people of that city?

Brasília

Create picture symbols for this map.

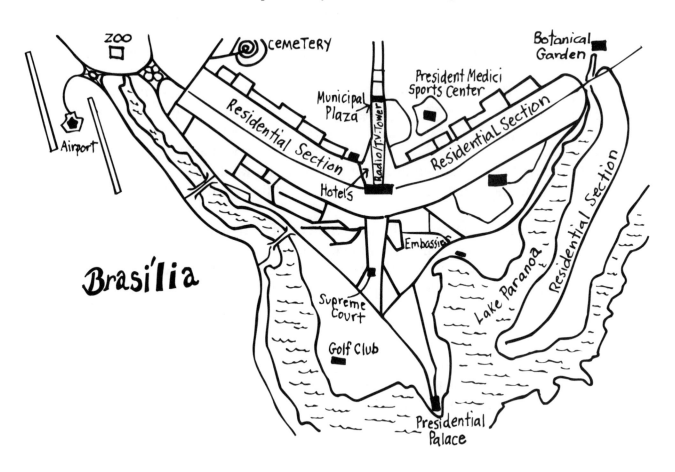

= Zoo

= Airport

= Cemetery

= Municipal Plaza

= Hotels

= Golf Club

= Radio/Television Tower

= Supreme Court

= Presidential Palace

= Embassies

= Residential Section

= Botanical Garden

= Sport Center

Chichén Itzá

Chichén Itzá was a city built about 1,500 years ago by the Mayan people. It is located on Mexico's Yucatán **Peninsula**, between the Gulf of Mexico and the Caribbean Sea.

The people believed that Chichén Itzá was a special place because it is the **site** of a large, **circular**, straight-sided well, called a *cenote*. The well is about 180 feet (55 m) across and 120 feet (37 m) deep. It is usually half-full of water, fed by rainfall and underground springs. This *cenote* was important because the Mayans believed their rain god, Chac, lived there.

If there was a **drought**, the people threw **sacrifices** of golden plates and jewelry, **jade**, pottery, or wooden **idols** into the well. They hoped to please Chac. If no rain came, they sometimes threw young men or women into the well. The people usually were drowned, but if they were able to stay alive long enough to be pulled from the water, the Mayans honored them as messengers from Chac.

The Spanish who conquered Mayan lands in the 1500s wanted the gold at the bottom of the "well of sacrifice," but they had no way of getting to it. An American named Edward Thompson spent 40 years exploring the ruins of Mayan cities. He hired local natives to **dredge** the well. At first they got nothing but mud, then just pieces of worthless, broken pottery. Thompson became discouraged. He continued the work for three years. Finally, he and his two assistants dove into the **muck** themselves. They found some items made of copper and bronze as well as some human bones, but little of real value. Thompson sent the items to Harvard University's Peabody Museum. That made the Mexican government angry. Many years after Thompson's death, the items were returned to Mexico.

Answer in complete sentences:

1. What should have been done with the artifacts from Chichén Itzá?

2. What did the Mayans sacrifice to the rain god Chac?

3. Describe the *cenote* at Chichén Itzá.

4. What were conditions like for Edward Thompson and his crew? Why did he continue working after so many discouraging attempts?

Web site:
www.realtime.net/maya/index.html

Science

You will need:

- ✔ nonfiction books about wells
- ✔ paper
- ✔ pencil

Learn how an underground well works. Draw a diagram showing how water is brought to the top.

Art

You will need:

- ✔ travel information about Mexico
- ✔ paper
- ✔ markers
- ✔ pencil

Design a tourist brochure for the Yucatán Peninsula.

Creative Writing

You will need:

- ✔ paper
- ✔ pencil

Write a letter from the Mexican government to the Peabody Museum asking for the return of the Chichén Itzá artifacts.

Social Studies

You will need:

- ✔ nonfiction books about Mayans
- ✔ paper
- ✔ pencil

Do research to learn more about the Mayan culture and their contributions to modern society.

Draw a map showing the areas where Mayans lived. Locate Chichén Itzá on Mexico's Yucatán Peninsula.

Chichén Itzá

Directions: Draw Chac and three items that might have been thrown into the sacrifice well. Explain your drawing.

The CN Tower

Located in Toronto, Canada, the CN (Canadian National) Tower is one of the tallest freestanding structures in the world. It is 1,815 feet (553 m) high, including the **antenna** at the top, and was completed in 1975. The Tower has four outside elevators, two observation platforms, a **revolving** restaurant, nightclub, **mini-theater**, exhibit **gallery**, and **microwave** broadcasting equipment. At ground level, there are high-tech rides and games.

One interesting feature of the CN Tower is an outdoor observation deck with a glass floor. It is possible to look through the floor 1,122 feet (342 m) straight down and see the ground. On the floor above, there is an indoor observation deck with **telescopes** and **periscopes**.

The mini-theater shows a film on the development and building of the CN Tower. In an area called the EcoDek, a visitor can watch **multimedia** exhibits about a variety of **environmental** problems. Thirty-three stories higher, from the world's highest public observation gallery, a visitor can see Lake Simcoe to the north and Niagara Falls to the south.

Answer in complete sentences:

1. What do you imagine you would see looking down through the glass-floored observation deck?

2. How do visitors climb the CN Tower?

3. What will a visitor to the Tower be able to see on a clear day?

4. What would you enjoy most about visiting the CN Tower?

Web site:
www.hype.com/toronto/attractions/cntower.htm

Research

You will need:

➤ nonfiction information about the Eiffel Tower
➤ paper
➤ pencil

Compare the Eiffel Tower and the CN Tower.

Science

You will need:

➤ nonfiction information about pollution and the environment
➤ paper
➤ pencil

What environmental problems are important to Canada? What are some possible solutions?

Creative Writing

You will need:

➤ nonfiction information about the CN Tower
➤ paper
➤ pencil

Write a news article that might have appeared in a local paper on the day of the opening of the CN Tower.

Social Studies

You will need:

➤ tourist information about Toronto
➤ paper
➤ pencil

Make a list of points of interest in the city of Toronto. Choose one and explain what you could expect to see if you paid a visit.

The CN Tower

Choose one of the structures pictured below. Read about it in an encyclopedia and write five facts to tell what you learned.

1. _____

   _____

2. _____

   _____

3. _____

   _____

4. _____

   _____

5. _____

   _____

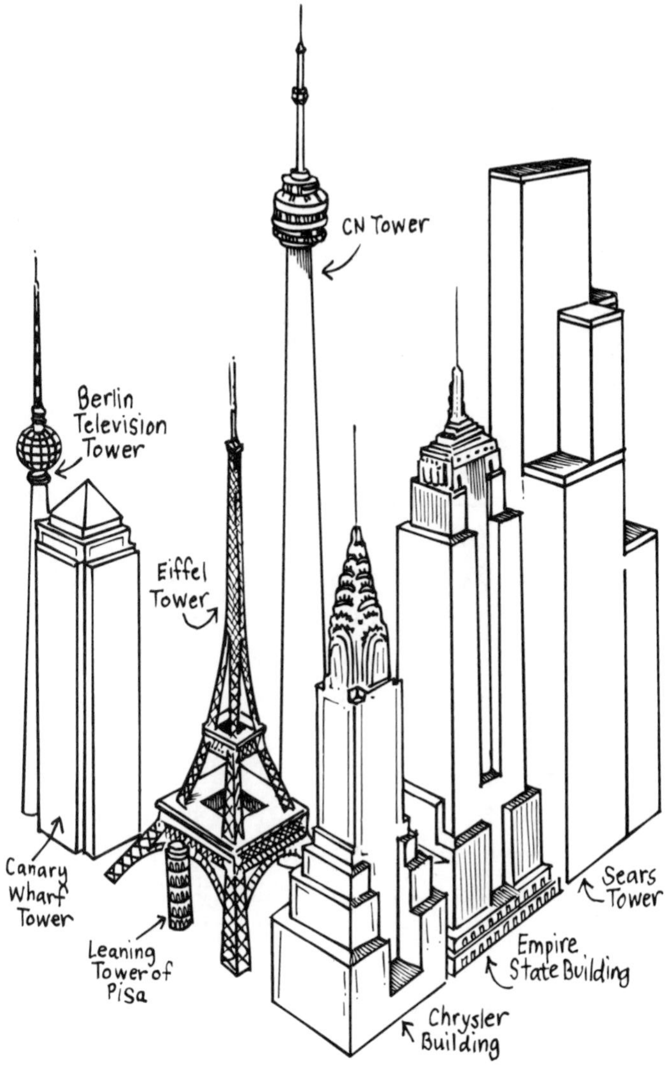

CN Tower

Berlin Television Tower

Eiffel Tower

Canary Wharf Tower

Leaning Tower of Pisa

Chrysler Building

Empire State Building

Sears Tower

Answer:

1. Which of the structures is the oldest? _____

   When was it built? _____

2. Which of the structures is the newest? _____

   When was it built? _____

3. Using what you have learned, how would you say tall structures have changed over the years?

   _____

   _____

Easter Island

The ancient statues (called *moai*) on Easter Island have fascinated explorers and archaeologists for centuries. In 1722, Admiral Jakob Roggeveen of the Dutch West India Company, "discovered" Easter Island and hundreds of gigantic stone statues in the shape of a human head and **torso.** Some of the statues were wearing caps carved from red stone. In 1774, when Captain James Cook arrived on the island, he found many of the statues had fallen from their positions and several were broken.

The triangular-shaped island, 2,300 miles (3,700 km) off the west coast of South America, is now owned by Chile. It has few plants and no trees. There is an **extinct** volcano at each corner of the island. The statues were created in the **crater** of one of these volcanoes. When "discovered" in the 1800s, the crater of Rano Raraku still held more than 200 unfinished statues. All of the heads had the same thin lips, large noses, and long earlobes. Archaeologists also found sculpting tools made of **obsidian** at the volcano site.

Little is known about the actual **origin** or meaning of the statues, though many people have **theories.** The well-known Norwegian explorer Thor Heyerdahl learned how the statues were moved and lifted into place from talking with a **descendant** of ancient islanders. Heyerdahl was able to **reenact** moving one of the statues, using more than 100 men pulling on ropes attached to a y-shaped tree-branch "sled." He also proved that it was possible to lift a statue into position by pushing three wooden poles under the face and using levers to raise the head. Stones were then pushed under the face and the backbreaking process was repeated until the statue was upright. The red hats were put in place using the same method.

Today, about 2,000 people, mostly Polynesians, live on Easter Island. Tourism and the export of wool are the main industries.

Answer in complete sentences:

1. What did Admiral Jakob Roggeveen and Captain James Cook "discover" at Easter Island?

2. Describe the statues found at Easter Island.

3. Explain how the statues were moved and put into position on the island.

4. How would modern sculptors make statues similar to those at Easter Island?

Web sites:
www.mysteriousplaces.com/Easter_Isld_Pge.html
www.netaxs.com/%7Etrance/rapanui.html

Social Studies

You will need:
- ✓ paper
- ✓ pencil
- ✓ nonfiction materials on Easter Island

Make five general statements about Easter Islanders considering the statues and the environmental conditions in which they live.

Art

You will need:
- ✓ white drawing paper
- ✓ charcoal or gray chalk

Make a drawing of the crater of Rano Raraku. Include several unfinished statues.

Creative Writing

You will need:
- ✓ drawing paper
- ✓ pencil
- ✓ markers

Fold the drawing paper in half. Label one side "before" and the other side "after." Write a story and make drawings that show the changes that may have taken place on Easter Island to accommodate the tourist industry.

Science

You will need:
- ✓ three unsharpened pencils
- ✓ two rulers
- ✓ a small statue (fairly heavy)
- ✓ several small rocks.

Demonstrate the Easter Islanders' method for raising the heavy statues by pushing the pencils under the statue and using the rulers as levers. The small rocks hold up the head.

Easter Island

Can You Solve The Mystery?

There are many ideas about the origin and meaning of the statues at Easter Island. Based on what you know, which theory do you believe is the most likely?

Could they have been

✦ burial sites?
✦ built by aliens?

✦ _____
(your theory)

Write information that supports your ideas.

_____

_____

_____

_____

_____

_____

_____

_____

_____

_____

Bonus: Debate your ideas with a friend. Try to persuade another student to your way of thinking.

_____

The Galapagos Islands

On March 10, 1535, Tomas de Berlanga and his crew spotted land as they sailed the Pacific Ocean. They hoped to find food and water. Instead, all they saw was black **lava**, stones, and cacti. The crew had "discovered" the Galapagos Islands.

Owned by the country of Ecuador, this group of 13 large and 6 smaller islands is now a national park. The islands are really the tops of volcanoes that exploded deep in the ocean more than a million years ago. The plants and animals that live on the Galapagos have **adapted** to conditions so that they can **survive** with little soil or water. The animals have no fear of people because the islands are so **isolated.**

The islands are named for the huge turtles, some weighing as much as 600 pounds, that live there. These giant **tortoises** live for many years eating cacti, grass, and shrubs. The **marine iguana** is the only iguana in the world able to live on seaweed and salt water. The only penguins adapted to life in the tropics are on the Galapagos.

The islands are home to many interesting sea birds that live nowhere else in the world. Charles Darwin, a famous scientist, found several kinds of **finches** on the islands. The birds had different kinds of beaks adapted for the foods they ate. Other sea birds include flightless **cormorants**, frigate birds, flamingoes, and boobies with blue feet.

Because they are fearless, the animals have fallen **prey** to people who have killed or captured them for museum collections or scientific study. Settlers and sailors brought new species to the island to breed. Many of those animals became wild and threatened the **native** animals. Today, scientists from around the world are working to protect the environment of the Galapagos Islands. There is a research station on the island of Santa Cruz where scientists work to breed **endangered** animals.

Answer in complete sentences:

1. Where are the Galapagos islands and who discovered them?

2. How were the islands created?

4. How has the marine iguana adapted to life on the islands?

5. Name five kinds of sea birds that live on the islands.

_____

Web site:
www.terraquest.com/galapagos/

Language Arts

You will need:
- ✓ paper
- ✓ pencil

Make a picture dictionary of ten animals or birds native to the Galapagos Islands.

Research

You will need:
- ✓ biography of Charles Darwin
- ✓ paper
- ✓ pencil

Explain the work of Charles Darwin on the Galapagos Islands. What theories did he have about the finches on the islands?

Name three other animals or plants that have adapted over the years to their environments. How has each one changed?

Art

You will need:
- ✓ nonfiction information about sea birds
- ✓ paper
- ✓ colored pencils

Draw one bird native to the Galapagos Islands, its habitat, and its food. Combine the pages in a class book of sea birds.

Do a similar project for an animal on the islands.

Science

You will need:
- ✓ encyclopedia (volume V)
- ✓ nonfiction information about volcanoes
- ✓ paper
- ✓ pencil

How are shield volcanoes formed?

Define magma, fumarole, lava, and caldera.

The Galapagos Islands

The animals and plants living on the Galapagos Islands are very special. They need to be protected from people who would do them harm. Make a list of rules that visitors must follow in order to protect the environment and the animals.

1. _____

2. _____

3. _____

4. _____

5. _____

How might the islands change in the next 20 years if people do not follow these rules today?

_____

_____

_____

_____

_____

_____

_____

_____

_____

_____

_____

_____

The Golden Gate Bridge

The Golden Gate Bridge and Highway District was formed on December 4, 1928, to supervise the construction of the Golden Gate Bridge. They chose Joseph B. Strauss to design the bridge, which **spans** the entrance to San Francisco Bay. Strauss believed that the bridge could pay for itself with **tolls.**

Work on the bridge began on January 5, 1933. For the first time, workers were required to wear special **head-gear** and **goggles.** They used hand and face creams to protect against the wind and ate a special diet to keep from becoming dizzy. A safety net was stretched under the floor of the bridge. The completed project was opened to the public on May 27, 1937.

The floor of the bridge is 90 feet (27 m) wide. It has a six-lane highway and sidewalks. The road sections of the bridge are designed to **sway** in a high wind. The structure has become known as one of the world's most **spectacular** bridges and is visited each year by thousands of tourists.

Answer in complete sentences:

1. Who was Joseph B. Strauss?

2. How did Strauss expect to pay for the bridge?

3. What was done to protect the construction workers on the bridge?

4. In what two ways do people cross the bridge?

Web site:
www2.goldengate.org/goldengate

Geography

You will need:

✔ map of San Francisco area
✔ pencil
✔ paper

Name six counties that form the Golden Gate Bridge and Highway District.

Social Studies

You will need:

✔ paper
✔ pencil

There are many types of bridges. Locate one in your community, make a drawing, and note the type of bridge.

Creative Writing

You will need:

✔ paper
✔ pencil

Write a first-person account of a day in the life of a bridge painter. What kinds of safety measures do the painters use? Why would it be a difficult job?

Research

You will need:

✔ nonfiction information about famous bridges of the world
✔ paper
✔ pencil

Write a paragraph about Humber Bridge in England. It is the world's longest suspension bridge. Draw a diagram.

Make a list of five famous bridges and the rivers they cross.

The Golden Gate Bridge

There are many types of bridges. Studies are made to determine who will use the bridge before a design is chosen.

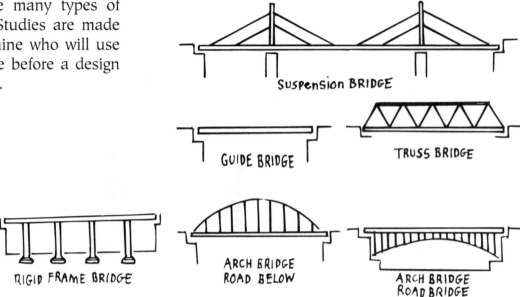

SUSPENSION BRIDGE

GUIDE BRIDGE

TRUSS BRIDGE

RIGID FRAME BRIDGE

ARCH BRIDGE ROAD BELOW

ARCH BRIDGE ROAD BRIDGE

Directions: Think of a bridge you have seen in your community or while traveling. Answer these questions.

1. Where is the bridge located? _____

2. The bridge is made of _____.

3. It is a _____ bridge.
                          (type)

4. What two points does it connect? _____ and _____

5. Circle one: The bridge is used by   **cars   pedestrians   both**

6. Did you cross this bridge? What did you see and hear?_____

_____

_____

Draw a picture of the bridge here:

The Grand Canyon National Park

The Grand Canyon National Park covers over one million acres, an area larger than the entire state of Rhode Island. The **canyon**, which makes up almost the entire area of the park, is about one mile (1.6 km) deep. It is the largest **gorge** in the world. It was formed over millions of years by the **erosion** of the Colorado River. In addition, changes in temperature and movements of the earth's **crust** made the gorge even deeper. A visitor can see layers of **sandstone**, **limestone**, **shale**, and other rocks on the canyon walls.

Elevations in the park range from 1,250 to 9,165 feet (381 m to 2,793 m). It is 18 miles (29 km) across at its widest point. There are huge differences in temperature and rainfall throughout the canyon. Deep in the canyon, it is hot and dry in the summer. Higher up, there is snow in the winter. The North Rim averages 10 feet (3 m) of snowfall each year. Because of the different climate zones, the park supports a variety of wildlife, including beavers, bighorn sheep, mountain lions, elk, lizards, and some 300 species of birds. There are 1,000 different species of flowering plants.

About four million visitors come to the park each year. They can drive on park roads, hike the trails, or enjoy the camping areas. Some tourists choose to ride mules along canyon trails or raft the Colorado River. The park also offers fishing and horseback riding, but hunting is prohibited. A small area of the park is set aside as a reservation for the Havasupai people who have lived along the Colorado River for centuries.

Answer in complete sentences:

1. How was the Grand Canyon formed?

2. What kinds of animals live in the park?

3. What activities are available for visitors to the park?

4. Explain how the elevations in the park affect the weather and wildlife.

Web sites:
www.thecanyon.com/nps/
www.kaibab.org:8000/gc/

Creative Writing

You will need:
- ✔ paper
- ✔ pencil

Write a story or journal about a camping trip to the park. Be sure to include information about activities, food, park rangers, and clothing necessary for the experience. Write a letter to request tourist information:

Superintendent, P.O. Box 129
Grand Canyon National Park
Grand Canyon, Arizona 86023

Science

You will need:
- ✔ samples of sandstone, limestone, shale, fossils
- ✔ clay
- ✔ sticks
- ✔ jar lids

Make animal footprints and leaf prints in clay that has been pressed and smoothed in jar lids.

Language Arts

You will need:
- ✔ markers
- ✔ chart paper
- ✔ outdoor magazines

Make a packing list for a week-long trip. Classify the items as food, clothing, or equipment. Draw or glue magazine pictures in each section.

Geography

You will need:
- ✔ a highway map of the Grand Canyon National Park area

Use the map of the Grand Canyon National Park. Label the North Rim, South Rim, Colorado River, Kaibab Plateau, and Walhalla Plateau.

The Grand Canyon National Park

Trace the route to the Grand Canyon from Phoenix, Arizona. Write the directions.

_____

_____

_____

Bonus (or alternate):
Trace the route to the Grand Canyon from Las Vegas, Nevada. Write the directions.

_____

_____

_____

Hoover Dam

Hoover Dam is in the Black Canyon of the Colorado River, just 25 miles (40 km) from Las Vegas, Nevada. It is part of the Boulder Canyon Project which was begun in 1928. Besides the dam, the project also included a **reservoir** and a **hydroelectric** power plant. The purpose of the dam is to control flooding on the Colorado River and supply water and electrical power to much of the Pacific Southwest.

Early in the 1900s, floods from the Colorado River caused damage to the Imperial and Palo Verde Valleys. **Levees** were built to control the river, but they were not successful and crops were lost. Congress approved the Boulder Canyon Project in 1928 at a cost of $385 million. The dam alone cost $175 million.

People from every part of the United States came to work on the dam. Many of them brought their families. Because times were hard and jobs were difficult to find during the Depression, these people were willing to live in tents or shacks along the river. They had no clean drinking water or toilets and little protection from harsh weather conditions. Many of them became sick and died. Some people were killed in construction accidents.

Hoover Dam, which controls the Colorado River, has created a **reliable** supply of water and **affordable** electricity for the people of the southwestern United States. It is 726 feet (221 m) high and 1,244 feet (379 m) long. The concrete base is 660 feet (201 m) thick. Lake Mead, the dam reservoir, provides water to cities in southern California and **irrigates** one million acres of farmland. **Generators** supply electrical power to much of Arizona.

The dam was renamed to honor President Herbert Hoover in 1931.

Answer in complete sentences:

1. What states have benefited from Hoover Dam? How does it help?

2. What is the purpose of the dam?

3. What is included in the Boulder Canyon Project besides the dam?

4. Why did Congress approve the Boulder Canyon Project in 1928?

5. What were living conditions like for the people who built the dam?

Web site:
www.hooverdam.com

Geography

You will need:

- ✔ nonfiction information about dams
- ✔ map of the United States
- ✔ pencil

Locate Hoover Dam and Lake Mead on the Arizona/Nevada border. Locate five nearby cities that benefit from the dam.

Mark the locations of five other major dams on your map.

Social Studies

You will need:

- ✔ nonfiction information about the Great Depression
- ✔ paper
- ✔ pencil

How were families and children affected by the Great Depression? What did they do to survive?

How did President Hoover try to solve the country's economic problems?

Creative Writing

You will need:

- ✔ paper
- ✔ pencil

How might the southwestern United States be different without Hoover Dam?

Write a diary entry of a child who camped at the Colorado River while his or her parent worked on the dam.

Research

You will need:

- ✔ encyclopedia (volume D)
- ✔ paper
- ✔ pencil

What materials are commonly used in building a dam?

When and where did American colonists build the first dam in the United States? What was its purpose?

Hoover Dam

Directions: Take a field trip to a dam in your area, or choose a dam from the list below and answer these questions.

1. Name of the dam: _____

2. Where is it located? _____

3. When was it built? _____ By whom? _____

4. Name of the river leading from the dam: _____

5. Name of the lake: _____

6. What is the primary purpose of the dam? (flood control, electric power, irrigation, etc.)

   _____

7. How did you get this information? _____

   _____

Wilson Dam   Grand Coulee Dam

St. Lawrence Dam   Roosevelt Dam

Cumberland Dam   Shasta Dam

Fort Peck Dam   Rio Grande Project

Draw a picture of the dam you selected.

Machu Picchu

The ancient city of Machu Picchu is located in the Andes Mountains in the South American country of Peru. It overlooks the Urubamba River. The city was built by the Inca, a group of people famous for their skill as builders. Very little is known about their reason for building Machu Picchu, but it is believed the city was built late in Incan history.

Although their **culture** was advanced, the Inca had no written language. What we know about them comes from studying the remains of their cities, **artifacts**, and graves. They worshiped the sun god, Init, and the name Inca means "children of the sun."

The city, covering five square miles (8 km), is well-planned with walled roads, stairways, and houses made of solid stone blocks. **Terraces** were carved from the mountainside for growing crops.

An **explorer** named Hiram Bingham "discovered" Machu Picchu on July 24, 1911. He and his group were led over a dangerous mountain trail by a local farmer. In a clearing they faced the city, which was 8,000 feet (2,438 m) above sea level between the **peaks** of Machu Picchu and Huayna Picchu. Bingham recorded what he saw in photographs and writing.

After clearing away the **brush** from the buildings, Bingham located the ruins of a structure built from white **granite** that he named the Temple of the Sun. He called Machu Picchu "the largest and most important ruin discovered in South America."

Answer in complete sentences:

1. Where is Machu Picchu located?

2. Who was Hiram Bingham and what did he do?

3. What group of South American people built Machu Picchu?

4. Describe Machu Picchu when Hiram Bingham found it.

Web sites:
www.realtime.net/maya/index.html
ftp.netgate.net/~lorna/machu.htm

Creative Writing

You will need:
- ✔ paper
- ✔ pencil
- ✔ markers or crayons

What ceremonies might have been held in the Temple of the Sun? Draw pictures to illustrate your ideas.

Art

You will need:
- ✔ art supplies (including clay, small stones, and modeling tools)

Design a clay model of Machu Picchu or create a diorama showing a scene from the daily life of the Inca.

Research

You will need:
- ✔ nonfiction information about South American natives
- ✔ encyclopedia (volume I)
- ✔ paper
- ✔ pencil

Report what you learned about the history of the Inca in South America.

How did the Inca cut and fit stones to make their buildings?

Social Studies

You will need:
- ✔ map of South America
- ✔ pencil

Locate Machu Picchu in the Andes Mountains of Peru. Estimate how many miles or kilometers it is from your home state. What path would you take to travel there? List the states and bodies of water you would cross.

Machu Picchu

Directions: How do you think the Incas would have adapted to life in the rain forest? How would that have been different than life at Machu Picchu? Complete this chart.

	Machu Picchu	Rain Forest
Tools		
Home		
Clothing		
Food		
Language		
Religion		

Mauna Loa

Located on the island of Hawaii, Mauna Loa is the largest active volcano in the world. Its **crater** rises 30,000 feet (9,144 m) from the ocean floor, making it taller than Mount Everest. The volcano is 60 miles (97 km) wide at its base. Scientists think that it **emerged** from the sea about 500,000 years ago. The last major **eruption** of Mauna Loa was in 1984. There is a much smaller, active volcano, Kilauea, nearby. A third volcano, Loihi, is still forming under the sea.

Mauna Loa's longest eruption lasted 18 months between 1855 and 1856. In 1926, lava destroyed a nearby fishing village and in 1984, it came within four miles of the city of Hilo.

The Hawaiian island volcanoes are formed when the ocean floor moves over a hot spot in the earth's **mantle**. When this happens, **molten** rock **erupts** lava onto the seabed. Over the years, many layers of this lava build up to form an underwater mountain. **Barriers** have been built on the island to contain the eruptions and protect the villages and cities that are in the path of volcanoes. In addition, scientists work to predict when eruptions will occur.

The Hawaii Volcanoes National Park, established in 1916, gives visitors the chance to stand on the **rim** of a crater and watch the volcanoes **spout geysers** of **molten lava**.

Answer in complete sentences:

1. How is a volcano formed?

2. How large is Mauna Loa?

3. Name the two smaller volcanoes near Mauna Loa.

4. What kinds of destruction can occur when a volcano erupts?

Web site:
volcano.und.nodak.edu/

Science

You will need:
- ✔ nonfiction books about volcanoes
- ✔ a map of the world
- ✔ pencil
- ✔ paper

Locate and label five other active volcanoes on the map of the world.

What is the job of a scientist who studies volcanoes? How are they trained? How do they help society?

Social Studies

You will need:
- ✔ nonfiction information about Hawaii
- ✔ paper
- ✔ pencil

How do the volcanoes affect the daily life of local people?

How do the volcanoes contribute to the beauty of the islands?

If you have visited Hawaii, share your photographs and experiences with the class.

Language Arts

You will need:
- ✔ dictionary
- ✔ encyclopedia (volume V)
- ✔ paper
- ✔ pencil

Define these terms: active, intermittent, dormant, extinct.

What is a shield volcano?

Research

You will need:
- ✔ encyclopedia (volumes P and M)
- ✔ paper
- ✔ pencil

What happened to the cities of Pompeii and Herculaneum when Mount Vesuvius erupted?

How was the area affected when Mount St. Helens erupted in 1980?

Mauna Loa

Directions: Look up these definitions in a dictionary. Draw or label them on the volcano diagram.

magma   fumarole   lava
caldera   mantle   crust

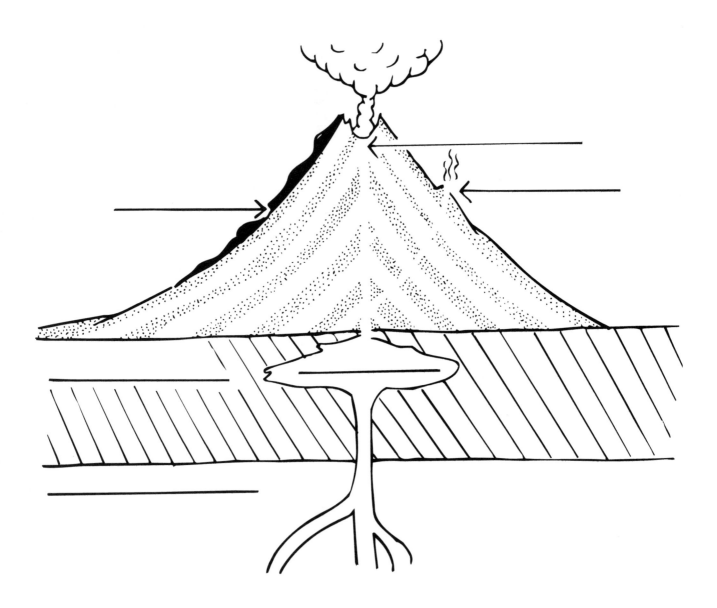

Mesa Verde

Native Americans called Anasazi (the ancient ones) came to live at Mesa Verde about 550 A.D. They farmed the flat-topped **mesa** and made their homes in **alcoves** in the cliffs of the **canyon** walls. They formed a strong community and produced pottery, tools, and baskets. The Anasazi grew beans, corn, and squash. They **vanished** from the area about 1300.

In 1888, Cliff Palace, the largest village ruin in Mesa Verde, was "discovered" by cowboys grazing their cattle. They found stone buildings, skeletons, and remains of baskets and pottery that proved people had once lived there.

Kivas, or round underground rooms, were built in front of the homes. These *kivas* were an important part of the Anasazi culture. There was a fire pit in the center of the floor and a hole in the roof for a ladder. Sometimes the *kiva* was entered through a tunnel. It is believed they were used for religious or healing ceremonies.

Archaeologists have unearthed the remains of buildings, fire pits, farming areas, and **shards** of pottery at Mesa Verde. Scientists can understand many things about the Anasazi from studying these remains. Medical experts can tell what kinds of diseases the people may have had. **Botanists** know what flowers and plants they grew. Geologists and **climatologists** study the land and the weather. Mesa Verde is the largest archaeological **preserve** in the United States.

For many years, the cliff dwellings of Mesa Verde were falling apart. Many people felt the government should find a way to protect the dwellings. President Theodore Roosevelt signed a bill making Mesa Verde a national park on June 2, 1906. Today, thousands of tourists visit five of the ruins each summer.

Answer in complete sentences:

1. What is the meaning of the Navajo word Anasazi?

2. What was found at Cliff Palace?

3. What have archaeologists found at Mesa Verde?

4. What has been done to help preserve the cliff dwellings at Mesa Verde?

5. What is a *kiva?*

Web site:
www.mesaverde.org/

Geography

You will need:
- ✔ map of the United States
- ✔ pencil

Circle the four corners area: Colorado, Utah, Arizona, and New Mexico where the cliff dwellings were found.

Art

You will need:
- ✔ modeling clay
- ✔ thin black or brown tempera
- ✔ fine paintbrush

Coil strips of clay in a circular pattern to make a bowl. Pinch the clay together to make the side walls and smooth the outside surface. Add a painted pattern to the outside.

Creative Writing

You will need:
- ✔ paper
- ✔ pencil

How would the cliff dwellings have protected the Anasazi from their enemies?

How would the cliff dwellings make them vulnerable?

Science

You will need:
- ✔ field guide of native plants
- ✔ paper
- ✔ pencil

Make a list of ten edible wild plants in your area.

Mesa Verde

Directions: Complete this chart:

How would droughts, storms, or floods have affected the quality of life for people at Mesa Verde?

	Drought	Storm	Flood
Food			
Crafts			
Travel			
Shelter			
Daily Activity			
Religion			

The Panama Canal

Cutting a **canal** through the **Isthmus** of Panama had interested people for many years. They wanted to save travel time and eliminate the dangerous trip around Cape Horn.

In 1882, the French began digging a sea level canal across the Isthmus. Their project failed because of poor management and disease. In 1889, the French gave up the project which was later taken over by the Americans.

In 1904, Americans decided to build a lock-and-lake canal, but knew they must first get rid of the mosquitoes that carried **yellow fever** and **malaria**. After ten years of hard work and $400 million, the canal was opened to international ship traffic.

A ship approaching from the Atlantic side passes through the Cristóbal Breakwater into Limón Bay where it waits to enter the canal. It next reaches and passes through the Gatun Locks and into Gatun Lake. The ship then follows a 23½ mile (38 km) **channel** to the Gaillard Cut, an 8 mile (13 km) trench cut through the solid rock and **shale** of the Continental Divide. Next, the ship enters the Pedro Miguel Locks that lead to Miraflores Lake and Miraflores Locks. From there it passes under the Bridge of the Americas into the Bay of Panama and Pacific Ocean.

The finished canal is 10 miles (16 km) wide and 50 miles (80 km) long, running between the Atlantic and Pacific Oceans. Each ship takes nine hours to travel from one end to the other. There is a railroad running the entire length of the canal which was used by engineers to haul earth to the **causeway** and dams.

There has been less ship traffic in the last ten years because many freighters are too large to pass through the canal. According to the Panama Canal Treaty, the United States government will turn the canal over to the Republic of Panama by the year 2000.

Answer in complete sentences:

1. Why did France fail to build the Panama Canal?

2. What diseases made digging the Panama Canal dangerous?

3. Why is the Panama Canal beneficial to trade?

4. What are the terms of the Panama Canal Treaty?

Web site:
holly.colostate.edu/~panama/section7.html

Research

You will need:
- ✓ encyclopedia (volume G)
- ✓ paper
- ✓ pencil

Write a summary of the work of George Washington Goethals (engineer) and William Gorgas (mosquito specialist).

Geography

You will need:
- ✓ map of the world
- ✓ paper
- ✓ colored pencils

Draw a map of the Americas. Mark the path ships take to pass through the Panama Canal from the Atlantic Ocean to the Pacific.

Science

You will need:
- ✓ nonfiction information about insects
- ✓ paper
- ✓ pencil

Explain how mosquitoes carry yellow fever and malaria. Draw and label a diagram of a mosquito.

Social Studies

You will need:
- ✓ encyclopedia (volume R) or a biography of Theodore Roosevelt
- ✓ paper
- ✓ pencil

Write a report on the presidency of Theodore Roosevelt. What did he have to do with building the Panama Canal?

The Panama Canal

Tracing the Journey

Read the article and trace the path of a ship
moving through the Panama Canal.

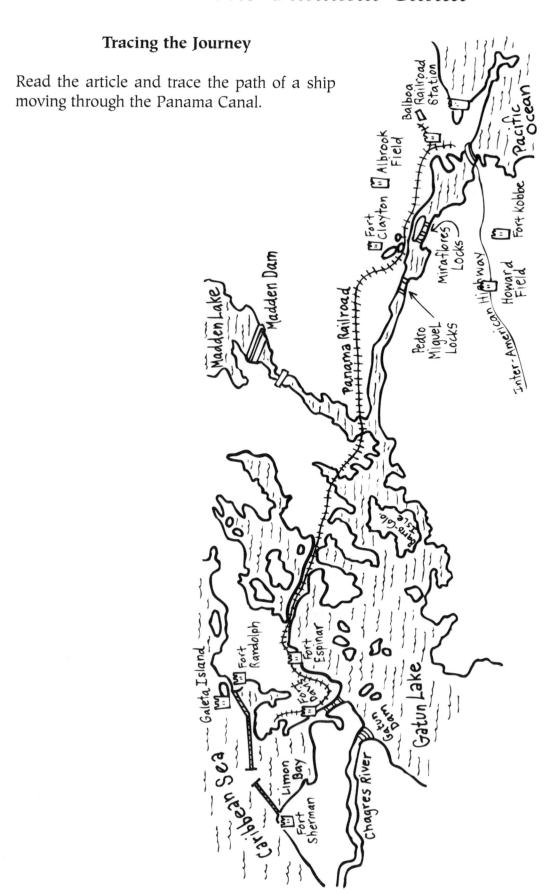

The Statue of Liberty

The Statue of Liberty is a symbol of **freedom** and friendship given to the people of the United States by the people of France. The statue has been standing on Bedloe's Island in New York Harbor since 1886.

The sculptor Frédéric-Auguste Bartholdi began with a small clay model and later made a one-quarter sized statue. The finished statue is 151 feet (46 m) tall, standing on a 65-foot (20 m) base, and an 89-foot (27 m) **pedestal**. Bartholdi wanted the statue to be strong enough for people to be able to walk inside and look out at the **harbor**.

Many artists, engineers, and **artisans** helped build Lady Liberty. She has a steel skeleton covered with **copper**. In her left hand, she holds a **tablet** bearing the date July 4, 1776, to **commemorate** the signing of the Declaration of Independence. Her right hand holds a lighted **torch** that welcomes **immigrants** to America. Liberty's crown has seven spikes that represent the seven seas and seven continents of the world. At her feet is a broken chain symbolizing the country's move to be free from Britain.

The finished statue was constructed in Paris, then taken apart and brought to the United States in 214 crates. It traveled by train and ship to America. Frédéric-Auguste Bartholdi **unveiled** his statue at a big celebration in the harbor filled with boats and ships. The Statue of Liberty stands today as the symbol of American independence and is visited by millions of people each year.

Answer in complete sentences:

1. Why was the Statue of Liberty given to the United States?

2. What are the dimensions of the Statue of Liberty?

3. Describe the meaning of each part of the Statue of Liberty: crown, right hand, left hand, and feet.

4. How was the Statue of Liberty brought to the United States?

Web site:
www.cityinsights.com/nystatue.htm

Social Studies

You will need:
- ✔ paper
- ✔ pencil
- ✔ encyclopedia

Research information about France's role in the war for independence between Britain and the United States.

Art

You will need:
- ✔ tagboard
- ✔ scissors
- ✔ ruler
- ✔ pencil
- ✔ stapler

Make a crown with a tagboard base and seven spikes stapled to the top edge. Fold the spikes forward.

Creative Writing

You will need:
- ✔ paper
- ✔ pencil

If you were an immigrant entering New York Harbor and seeing the Statue of Liberty for the first time, how would you feel?

Social Studies

You will need:
- ✔ tourist information about New York City
- ✔ 4" x 6" (10.2 x 15 cm) plain white cards

Make a list of other New York landmarks. Choose one to research in depth and report back to the class. Use the tourist information to design a bulletin board.

The Statue of Liberty

Crayon Resist Picture

You will need:
white drawing paper
crayons
craft stick or toothpick

Directions:
Cut and glue the Statue of Liberty to the white paper.

Apply large areas of several bright crayon colors around the statue.

Cover the bright colors with a heavy black crayon.

Use a craft stick or toothpick to chip away the black crayoning in star-burst shapes to reveal fireworks in the night sky around the statue.

Tenochtitlán

Tenochtitlán was the center of the Aztec Empire for almost 200 years. It was built on the site of present-day Mexico City. Legend says that Huitzilopochtli, the Aztec sun god, told the Aztec people to settle in a place where they found an eagle grasping a snake, perched on a cactus. In 1325, they found such a sign at Lake Texcoco. Huitzilopochtli became the **patron** god of the city.

Tenochtitlán grew into a powerful city-state, controlling much of the region. An **alliance** was formed with two other cities in the area, Texcoco and Tlacopan. Tenochtitlán was the largest and most powerful member of the alliance. There was no money system, so **merchants** traveled throughout the **empire** trading such goods as cacao beans, cotton, rubber, and **pelts** for a variety of manufactured products. Because the Aztecs only used the wheel in toys, all travel was done on foot or by water. The empire grew under the leadership of Montezuma I (1440–1469).

Over 150,000 people lived at Tenochtitlán by 1500. They lived in stone houses and built temples and palaces. They reclaimed the land by **dredging** mud from the lake bottoms. Tenochtitlán was a city of **canals** linked to the **mainland** by raised **footpaths**. The empire continued to grow under Montezuma II.

In 1519, Spanish explorer Hernando Cortés and his soldiers marched on the Aztec capital. They destroyed most of the Aztec architecture. Hundreds of years later, the Great Temple of Tenochtitlán was **excavated** in Mexico City. Archaeologists have unearthed some 6,000 objects including pottery, jewelry, carvings, and human remains. The Mexican government has rebuilt an Aztec **pyramid** near Mexico City.

Answer in complete sentences:

1. What three cities formed the Aztec alliance?

2. Explain the Aztec system of trade.

3. What were the results of the Spanish conquest in 1519?

4. Why did the Aztecs choose to live in areas with many lakes and canals?

5. What items were found in the excavations of the Great Temple?

Web sites:
www.realtime.net/maya/index.html
pharos.bu.edu/Egypt/Wonders/Forgotten/tenochtitlan.htm

Research

You will need:
- ✔ encyclopedia (volume P)
- ✔ paper
- ✔ pencil

Compare and contrast Aztec, Egyptian, and Mayan pyramids.

Art

You will need:
- ✔ a variety of art supplies

Design your idea of an Aztec sun god.

Draw an eagle grasping a snake perched on a cactus.

Language Arts

You will need:
- ✔ a Spanish/English dictionary
- ✔ paper
- ✔ pencil

Make a list of five Spanish words and list their English meanings. Memorize the words. Teach your words to a classmate until she or he has also memorized them.

Social Studies

You will need:
- ✔ travel information about Mexico City
- ✔ paper
- ✔ pencil

Plan a week-long trip to Mexico City. Include travel costs and a packing list. What special considerations are necessary when traveling in a foreign country? What sights will you see?

Tenochtitlán

Archaeologists have discovered information about Tenochtitlán under present-day Mexico City. Use an atlas and an encyclopedia to discover this information about the Mexican capital.

Answer five of these questions:

1. What is the current population of the city?

   _____

   _____

2. What are housing problems facing the people of Mexico City?

   _____

   _____

3. What is the Palacio de Belles Artes?

   _____

   _____

4. What is the most popular mode of transportation in the city?

   _____

   _____

5. What is Chapultepec Park?

   _____

   _____

6. How are the roads arranged throughout the city?

   _____

   _____

7. What are two typical industries or businesses of the city?

   _____

   _____

8. How has the city dealt with the problems of overpopulation?

   _____

   _____

9. What universities are located in Mexico City?

   _____

   _____

10. What is the Zócalo?

   _____

   _____

Reference List

Belt, Don. 1992. The World's Greatest Lake. *National Geographic*. June, Vol. 181, No. 6. p. 2. (partial nudity)

Carrier, Jim. 1992. Gatekeepers of the Himalaya. *National Geographic*. December, Vol. 182, No. 6. p 70.

Conniff, Richard. 1993. Easter Island Unveiled. *National Geographic*. March, Vol. 183, No. 3. p. 54.

Gore, Rick. 1991. Ramses the Great. *National Geographic*. April, Vol. 179, No. 4. p. 2.

Grove, Noel. 1992. Volcanos: Crucibles of Creation. *National Geographic*. December, Vol. 182, No. 6. p. 5.

Jordan, Robert Paul. 1987. New Zealand: the Last Utopia? *National Geographic*. May, Vol. 171, No. 5. p. 654.

Lehner, Mark. 1991. Computer Rebuilds the Ancient Sphinx. *National Geographic*. April, Vol. 179, No. 4. p 32.

Mitchell, John, G. 1994. Our National Parks. *National Geographic*. October, Vol. 186, No. 4. p. 2.

Newcott, William, R. 1993. The Living Tower of London. *National Geographic*. October, Vol. 184, No. 4. p. 36.

Payne, Oliver. 1995. Koalas Out on a Limb. *National Geographic*. April, Vol. 187, No. 4. p. 36.

Roberts, David. 1995. Age of Pyramids: Egypt's Old Kingdom. *National Geographic*. January, Vol. 187, No. 1. p. 2.

Roberts, David. 1996. The Old Ones of the Southwest. *National Geographic*. April, Vol. 189, No. 4. p. 86.

Stanfield, James, L. 1989. The New, the Enduring Paris. *National Geographic*. July, Vol. 176, No. 1. p. 6.

Theroux, Peter. 1997. The Imperiled Nile Delta. *National Geographic*. January, Vol. 191, No. 1. p.2.

Van Dyk, Jere. 1995. Amazon: South America's River Road. *National Geographic*. February, Vol. 187, No. 2 p. 2.

Zwingle, Erla. 1995. More than a Dream: Venice. *National Geographic*. February, Vol. 187, No. 2. p. 73.

Uluru (Ayer's Rock)—page 43

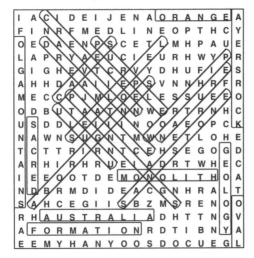

The Waiotapu Thermal Wonderland—page 85

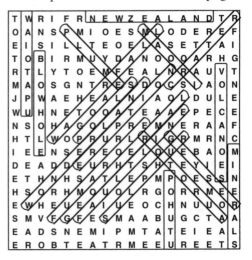

The Channel Tunnel—page 92

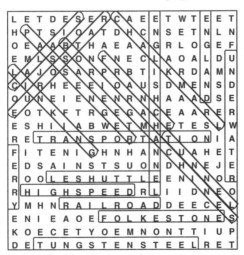

The Eiffel Tower—page 98

The Kremlin—page 104

Stonehenge—page 116

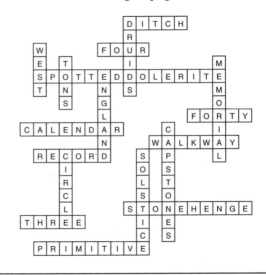